CUT IT OFF BOOK

Letting go Notebook

A Helpful Self-Healing Guided Journal for Women

Clara Hamilton

25 COVER COLOR OPTIONS

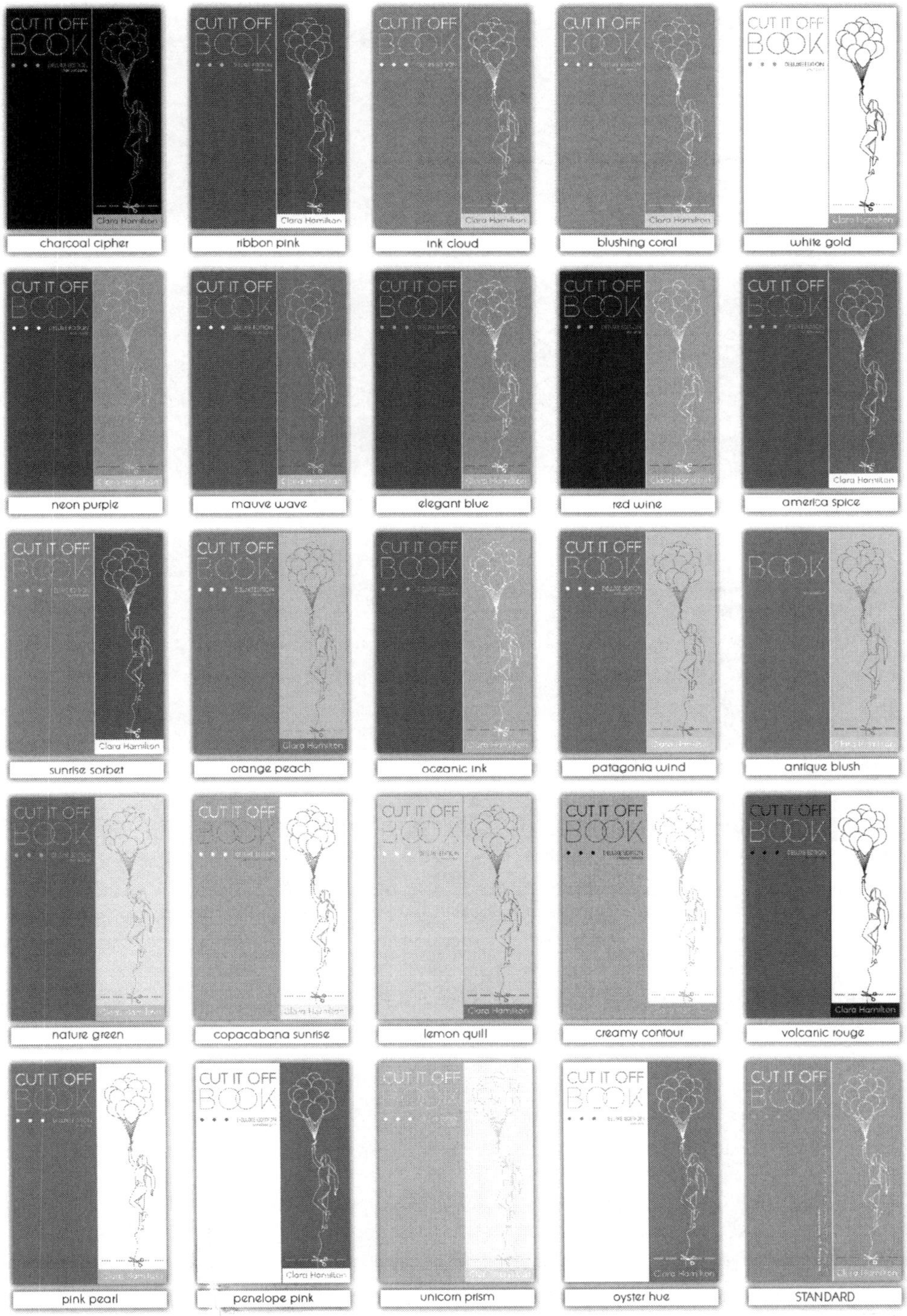

CUT IT OFF BOOK

Letting Go Notebook

A Helpful Self-Healing
Guided Journal for Women

By Clara Hamilton
www.clara-hamilton.com

Editorial services by Octagonal Press LTD
Cover design, interior layout, and formatting by AphantasiaLabs.com

ISBN: 9781917754033

VISIT OCTAGONAL PRESS ONLINE

Published by:
Octagonal Press LTD
128 City Road
London
EC1V 2NX

www.octagonalpress.com
info@octagonalpress.com

First Edition: 2025

Disclaimer

Hey ***beautiful***,

I just want to pause for a moment and talk straight from the heart—because if you're here right now, holding this journal, it means you're ready for something new, something fresh, something wonderful. So let me dedicate this little love note:

To every incredible woman who has ever felt stuck, overwhelmed, or tangled up in something that no longer serves her—you are brave beyond words for showing up, right here, right now.

To you, my dear friend, who sometimes forgets just how powerful and worthy you truly are—this book is your safe space, your cozy corner, your coffee date with a friend (yep, that's me!), and your personal guide to gently letting go of whatever has been weighing you down.

This journal isn't just pages and prompts—it's your permission slip to reclaim your joy, rediscover your glow, and step boldly toward the happiness you deserve. Whether you're releasing a painful past, saying goodbye to toxic relationships, or simply creating space for more of what lights you up—I am right here, holding your hand, cheering you on every step of the way.

I'm so incredibly proud of you for taking this courageous step. Remember, you're never alone on this journey. We're doing this together, one heartfelt page at a time.

With all my love, hugs, and endless support,

Clara Hamilton

Table of Contents

0

Introduction

Hi friend, and welcome. I'm Clara Hamilton, and I'm so happy you're here with me. I want you to imagine that we're just two friends sitting together—maybe curled up on a cozy couch with a cup of coffee—having a heart-to-heart chat. That's exactly how I want this introduction (and this journal) to feel for you: warm, personal, and real. Before we dive in, let me share a little story from my life and why I created this guided journal. I promise, this isn't going to be a stiff, formal introduction. It's just me, Clara, talking to you, one friend to another, about learning to let go of the bad stuff and invite in the good.

My Story of Letting Go

On the outside, my life might have looked pretty perfect. I grew up in sunny Newport Beach, in a loving (and yes, wealthy) family. I had a great education, amazing opportunities, and long blonde hair I was very proud of. You'd think with all that, I'd have zero problems, right? But inside, I often struggled with self-doubt and the pressure to be perfect. I was the friend who never said "no," the girl who smiled and agreed even when my heart was heavy. I felt I had to be kind and pleasing all the time, even if it meant holding onto relationships and habits that secretly hurt me.

Let me tell you about one night, a couple of years ago, that changed everything. I was 23 and had just gone through a really tough breakup. I had been in a relationship with someone I thought I'd marry someday. In reality, he often made me feel small and unworthy—like no matter what I did, I was never enough. After one especially painful argument over the phone, I remember sitting on my bedroom floor, tears streaming down my face. All the negative things I believed about myself came crashing down on me. I felt stuck—stuck in heartache, stuck in anger, stuck in a version of myself I didn't want to be. That's when something inside me just... snapped (in a good way). I stood up, went to the bathroom mirror, and stared at this girl with puffy eyes who I barely recognized. In a surge of emotional clarity, I reached for a pair of scissors on the counter. With trembling hands and a pounding heart, I gathered my long, tangled hair and **snip!** I cut it off—six, maybe eight inches of it. Blonde strands fell to the counter and floor. I know it sounds crazy, but with each cut, I felt like I was cutting away months of sadness and self-doubt that had been weighing me down.

In that moment, I felt free for the first time in ages. Of course, chopping off my hair didn't instantly heal my broken heart (my stylist was shocked the next day, to say the least!). But it was a symbolic action—a promise to myself that I would start cutting off more than just split ends. I was going to cut off the negativity in my life: the toxic relationships, the habit of saying "yes" to everyone but myself, and the inner voice that told me I wasn't good enough. That night marked the beginning of my self-healing journey.

The very next day, I grabbed the journal my sister had given me (just a simple notebook at the time) and started writing. I poured out everything: the hurt, the anger, the relief, the hope I felt creeping back in. It was like talking to a trusted friend—no judgments, no filters. I wrote about how much I gave in that relationship and how little I got back. I scribbled down the fears that kept me up at night: fear of being alone, fear of not being loved, fear of failing. And as I wrote, something amazing happened. With each page I filled, I felt a little lighter, a little more empowered. It was as if every word I wrote was helping me cut one of the thin, invisible strings tying me to the pain. Day by day, page by page, I was **letting go**.

Over the next weeks and months, journaling became my personal therapy. If I felt angry, I'd write a fiery letter in my journal to the person who hurt me (I never sent it, of course—it was just for me). If I felt sad or insecure, I'd jot down every single worry and then respond to myself with the kind words I'd offer a good friend. I started noticing patterns in my writing—like how I always apologized for everything, or how I held onto guilt from things that weren't my fault. And then, I began using my journal to gently challenge those patterns. Why was I so afraid to put myself first? Why did I keep toxic friendships alive just because I feared hurting others by leaving? The more I wrote, the more I understood that **cutting off** negativity wasn't an act of cruelty or giving up; it was an act of *self-love*.

Fast-forward to today: While I definitely don't have everything figured out (who does?), I'm in such a better place. I trimmed away the relationships that made me feel less than worthy. I said goodbye to some bad habits (bye-bye, late-night doom-scrolling and comparing myself to strangers on the internet!). And most importantly, I've made space in my heart and my life for things that truly matter and bring me joy. I feel more confident, passionate, and alive than I ever thought possible. And guess what? Journaling was (and still is) one of my biggest tools for getting here.

How This Journal Will Help You

I wanted to share that story with you because it taught me something life-changing: when we cut off the negative energy, habits, people, or thoughts that hold us back, we create room for better things to grow. That's exactly the purpose of *Cut It Off Book: Letting go Notebook—A Helpful Self-Healing Guided Journal for Women*. I created this journal as a safe, welcoming space for you to start your own journey of letting go and self-discovery, just like I did. Think of it as your personal refuge, a place where you can be honest about what's weighing you down and then gently release it. And don't worry, you won't be doing this alone—I'll be right here in these pages with you, guiding you like a close friend who wants nothing but the best for you.

What can you expect from this journal? Inside, you'll find a collection of guided prompts, heartfelt advice, and creative exercises that I've curated from my own healing process. Each section of the journal is designed to help you peel back the layers and get to the heart of what you need to cut off. We'll walk through various aspects of life—self-esteem, relationships, habits, and emotional baggage—and work on them one by one. Some prompts will invite you to reflect on your past and identify any toxic ties or patterns holding you back. Others will encourage you to dream and imagine the beautiful life you want to make space for. You might laugh at some points and cry at others (totally okay, I've done both!). Along the way, I've sprinkled in some of my favorite uplifting quotes and positive affirmations to cheer you on, because everyone needs a little pep talk now and then.

Throughout *Cut It Off*, I'll ask you to do something very important: be kind to yourself. Self-healing isn't always a straight line; it can be messy, emotional, and challenging. But it's **worth it**—and you deserve to feel happy and whole. This journal is here to guide you, but you are the one doing the brave work. Every time you put pen to paper and tell your truth, you're taking a step toward freeing yourself from whatever has been holding you down. Consider each writing prompt like a friendly nudge or a pair of scissors (the gentle, safety kind ✂) to help you snip away at that tangle of negativity in your life.

To give you a little preview, as you work through this journal you will be gently guided to:

- **Identify** the people, habits, or thoughts that drain your energy or bring you down. *(Who or what have you outgrown? What negative voices—even your own inner critic—do you need to turn off?)*

- **Reflect** on why these things took root in your life and what you truly feel about them. *(How did they get here, and what have they been costing you emotionally?)*

- **Cut off and release** the negativity with compassion and firmness. *(You'll find exercises to help you symbolically let go — think of writing a goodbye letter you never send, or imagining yourself clipping a thread that connects you to a bad memory.)*

- **Make space** for healing, positive energy and new beginnings. *(We'll explore what you want to invite into that fresh, open space—maybe it's self-confidence, healthier relationships, or simply peace of mind.)*

By the end of this journal, my hope is that you'll feel **lighter**, **stronger**, and more **empowered** in your life. You'll have clearer boundaries about what (and who) you allow into your world. You'll celebrate the growth you've achieved, and you'll carry forward the tools and insights to keep nurturing yourself long after you've filled these pages. In short, you'll have cut off what doesn't serve you to make room for what truly lights you up.

Before we jump in, I want you to know one more thing: **you are not alone**. Whatever you're facing right now, however big or small your struggles feel, I'm here with you in spirit, cheering you on. I wrote this journal because I genuinely care—I know the pain of holding onto things that hurt, and I also know the joy and relief of finally letting them go. Consider this book as a hug in written form, a judgment-free zone where you can be honest and kind to yourself. Let it be your companion on days when you feel strong and on days when you need extra support.

Alright, my friend. It's time. Time to pick up your pen, open your heart, and begin the beautiful work of cutting off the negativity and planting something new and wonderful in its place. I am so proud of you for taking this step toward your own healing. You deserve the happiness and freedom that await you on the other side of this journey. Let's do this together, one page at a time.

I give myself permission
to walk away from
what weighs me down.

1

Embracing Where You Are

Starting a new journey can feel both exciting and intimidating. I want you to know that whatever you're feeling right now is completely normal. In this chapter, we're going to take things step by step—together. By the end of it, you'll have a clearer understanding of where you stand and feel more confident about the path ahead.

Just as a tiny seedling bravely pushes through the darkness, you too are making a brave start by embarking on this journey. It might not look like much progress yet, and that's okay. Every great accomplishment begins with the decision to try—and that's exactly what you're doing. This seemingly small step you're taking today is actually a powerful leap toward a brighter future.

Acknowledging Your Feelings and Experiences

Before we map out where you want to go, let's pause and recognize where you are right now. Take a moment to acknowledge your feelings and experiences up to this point. Are you hopeful, nervous, unsure, or maybe a mix of everything? Whatever the feelings are, *they are valid*. Many experts emphasize that honestly acknowledging our emotions is the first step toward meaningful change. By naming what you feel—be it excitement or fear—you're allowing yourself to truly face it, rather than pushing it aside.

I understand it might be uncomfortable to dwell on difficult feelings. You might worry that focusing on fears or doubts could make them more real. But in reality, giving yourself permission to feel and express these emotions can be incredibly freeing. In fact, psychological research suggests that accepting our emotions (instead of fighting them) can reduce their intensity and impact. In other words, when you acknowledge a fear, you often take away some of its power over you.

Remember Why You Started

Every journey begins with a reason. Maybe you're seeking clarity, healing, personal growth, or something else entirely. Whatever brought you here, acknowledging it can help guide you forward and remind you why this effort is worthwhile.

A gentle way to explore where you are right now is through reflection. Take a quiet moment for yourself, grab your pen, and write freely—without judgment. Be honest with yourself; this is your space to understand yourself better.

• • •

Why did you decide to start this journaling journey, and what do you hope to gain from it?

What excites me about starting this journey? —*Every new beginning has something that lights a spark. What is it for you?*

What fears or concerns do I have right now? —*It's okay to have worries. Naming them can help you understand and address them in time.*

What past experiences might be influencing how I feel? – Sometimes our history (like past attempts or challenges) can echo in our current mindset. Recognizing this can help you be kinder to yourself.

What do I hope to achieve or change? – Deep down, what is calling you to take this journey? It's fine if it's a fuzzy idea; just note whatever comes to mind.

There are no right or wrong answers here. This exercise is simply about understanding yourself. By reflecting on these questions, you're building self-awareness—a crucial foundation for growth. And remember, you don't have to share these reflections with anyone. This is your safe space to be open and honest with yourself.

Understanding Self-Worth and Self-Acceptance

Self-love isn't just a *buzzword*—it's truly the foundation of a healthy, joyful life. But what does it really mean to love yourself? At its heart, self-love is about recognizing your own inherent worth and treating yourself with the same kindness and respect that you offer to people you care about. It means accepting yourself—**all of yourself**—just as you are right now, while also caring enough to grow and heal where you need to.

For so many of us *(especially women)*, practicing self-love can feel really tough. We've often been taught to put others first and might even feel guilty when we focus on ourselves. We might worry that self-love is selfish or vain. But here's the truth: taking care of yourself allows you to take better care of everything and everyone in your life. It's like the airplane oxygen mask analogy - you have to put on your own mask before you can help someone else with theirs. You absolutely deserve the same compassion that you so freely give to friends, family, and even strangers.

I want you to know that your worth isn't something you have to earn—you were born worthy. Self-acceptance means acknowledging your strengths and your flaws, and loving yourself not in spite of those imperfections but even because of them! It's understanding that you are enough, exactly as you are. When you embrace this truth, something amazing happens: you start to feel more at peace, more confident, and more resilient. Loving yourself becomes a source of strength that can carry you through even the toughest times.

Now, I know that simply saying *"love yourself"* is easier said than done. Truly loving yourself is a journey, not a one-time decision. It starts with small steps and little moments of reflection. So let's take one of those steps together now.

Reflection & Journaling Prompts

Take a moment to pause and reflect on how you feel about self-love and self-worth. Grab a pen and be open as you write. Remember, there's no judgment here. Use the space below to write freely from your heart.

• • •

What negative or critical things do you often think or say about yourself? How do these thoughts usually make you feel?

Think of a quality, talent, or something you have done that you feel proud of or appreciate about yourself. Why is this meaningful to you, and how does it feel to acknowledge it?

In your own words, what does "loving yourself" really mean to you? Try to describe how it might feel to completely accept yourself, with all of your beautifully human imperfections.

The "Cut It Off" Release

One of the most powerful steps in building self-love is learning to let go of the negative thoughts that weigh us down. By now, you might have written down some painful beliefs or harsh self-criticisms in the prompts above. Soon, we're going to *"cut them off"*—literally and symbolically—to help release the hold they have over you. But not now! Not yet. We'll get to this *"ritual"* in the next chapter.

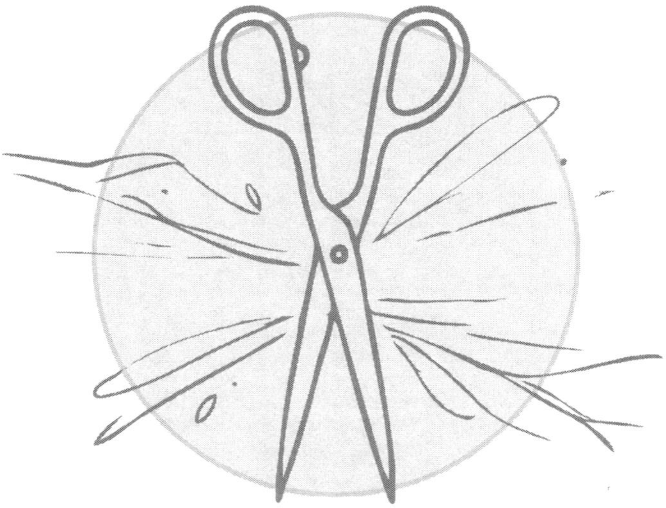

Setting Your Intentions and Goals

Once you've acknowledged how you feel at the start, the next step is to gently set an intention for where you want to go. Think of your intention as your guiding star—it gives you a sense of direction and meaning, but it isn't a rigid, unchangeable decree. In a warm, conversational way: why are you here? What do you hope this journey brings into your life?

Research has shown that when we have personal, meaningful reasons behind our goals, we're more likely to stay motivated and see them through. In other words, connecting your goals to your heart makes them stronger. For example, saying *"I want to get fit because I value my health and want to play with my kids without getting tired"* is more powerful than just *"I should lose weight because I feel I have to."* One is guided by personal meaning, the other by external pressure.

Take a moment to imagine what a positive outcome looks like for you. It could be big or small, concrete or abstract. Maybe you envision yourself feeling confident speaking up at work, or perhaps you see yourself waking up with more energy and less stress. You might have more than one intention - that's perfectly fine. To spark some ideas, here are a few examples of personal intentions:

- *"I want to improve my communication skills so I can build stronger relationships."*
- *"I intend to take better care of my health, so I feel happier and more energetic each day."*
- *"I want to learn new skills to advance my career and feel proud of my accomplishments."*
- *"My goal is to understand and manage my emotions better, so I can handle challenges with calm and clarity."*

Your own intentions will be unique to you. They don't have to sound profound or perfect. The key is that they matter to **you**. Write them down or say them out loud. Keep them somewhere you can revisit, especially on days when motivation feels low. Having this guiding star can remind you *why* you started when the journey gets challenging.

And remember, it's okay if your goals evolve as you do. This journey is not a straight line. As you learn and grow, you might discover new priorities or paths. That's all part of the process. The important thing right now is that you have a starting focus—a hopeful vision to move toward.

Starting Small and Staying Consistent

With your feelings acknowledged and your intentions set, you might be feeling eager to get going—which is wonderful! Enthusiasm can be a great fuel. But here's a gentle reminder: you don't have to *(and usually can't)* do everything all at once. In fact, one of the kindest and most effective things you can do for yourself is to **start small**.

Why start small? Because small steps, taken consistently, lead to big changes over time. Think of it this way: it's better to walk steadily at a pace you can maintain than to sprint quickly and burn out after a short distance. Research in habit-building supports this idea - making tiny, manageable changes and repeating them is more likely to create lasting habits. Plus, each small step you take gives you a little victory, a boost of confidence that *"Yes, I can do this."*

You might have a big end-goal in mind, and that's great. But consider breaking it down into bite-sized actions. For example, if your intention is to get healthier, a small step might be adding one extra glass of water to your day, or taking a 10-minute walk in the mornings. If you want to advance your career, perhaps a small step is reading one article each day about your field or reaching out to a mentor for a brief chat. These may seem like modest actions, but they are the building blocks of progress.

Here are a few examples of starting small, depending on your goals:

- If you aim to exercise regularly, begin with a simple routine like 5-10 minutes of stretching or walking each day, rather than jumping into a heavy workout plan immediately.
- For improving your diet, you could start by adding just one serving of vegetables to one meal a day, or swapping out soda for water a few times a week.
- Want to develop a new skill? Commit to practicing it for just 15 minutes each evening. Consistency matters more than the initial intensity or duration.
- If you're trying to reduce stress, start a habit of taking two or three deep breaths at a set time each day, or jotting down one thing you're grateful for before bed.

Each of these actions might seem small on their own, but over weeks and months, they add up significantly. More importantly, **they are achievable**, even on days when you're busy or not feeling your best. By accomplishing a small step, you reinforce a positive belief: *I can do this*. Over time, you can always add more or ramp up your efforts once the small steps become part of your routine.

It's also important to celebrate these small victories. Did you drink that extra glass of water today? Great! Give yourself credit for it. Finished a 10-minute walk? Fantastic—that's progress. By acknowledging these mini-achievements, you keep your morale high and make the journey enjoyable. Psychologists have found that celebrating small wins can boost your mood and motivation, making it more likely you'll continue with your new habits.

Of course, there might be days when even the small steps feel hard. Maybe you'll skip a day or something will interrupt your new routine - and that's okay. It doesn't mean you've failed or that you should give up. It just means you're human. On those days, be kind to yourself (remember, you're acknowledging feelings without judgment) and pick up again when you can. Consistency isn't about being perfect; it's about always coming back, repeatedly choosing to continue your journey.

Affirmations for Confidence & Worthiness

To wrap up this chapter, I want to share some powerful affirmations. These are positive statements you can repeat to yourself to reinforce the truth of your worth and boost your confidence. Speak them out loud in the morning or write them on sticky notes where you'll see them. Pick one or two that really resonate with you, or use them all—whatever feels right.

- *I am worthy of love and respect, exactly as I am.*
- *I am enough.*
- *I treat myself with compassion and kindness.*
- *I release self-criticism and choose self-love instead.*
- *I am proud of the person I am becoming.*
- *I deserve the same care and attention that I give to others.*
- *I embrace my imperfections, for they make me unique and beautiful.*

Let these affirmations soak in. Repeat them often, especially if that old critical voice creeps up again. Over time, statements like *"I am worthy"* won't just be words -—ey will become feelings you carry in your heart.

Looking Ahead: You've Got This

Take a moment to appreciate how far you've come in just this first chapter. You took the courageous step to begin, you opened up to your own feelings, set personal intentions, and learned the value of starting small. That's a lot of groundwork laid—and it's something to be proud of.

I want to reassure you that feeling a mixture of hope and uncertainty at this point is completely normal. Every journey worth taking has its early jitters and its *"am I really doing this?"* moments. But here you are, actively engaging, reflecting, and planning. By doing that, you've already distinguished yourself from those wishes that never leave the realm of day-dreams. You're making it real, one step at a time.

As we move on, keep your intentions and those small steps in mind. They are your compass and your engine. Whenever you feel lost or discouraged later, you can return to what you wrote down in this chapter—your feelings, your why, and the tiny actions you committed to. They will remind you of the path and give you the strength to continue.

In the next part of our journey, we'll build upon this foundation. Each chapter will guide you through new challenges and discoveries, but the supportive tone and clarity will remain the same. You are not alone in this—I'm here with you in these pages, and many others have walked similar paths, feeling what you feel. Together, we'll navigate the ups and downs.

For now, take a deep breath and give yourself credit for completing Chapter 1. This is only the beginning, and already you are growing. Whenever you're ready, let's turn the page and see what Chapter 2 has in store.

Remember: **you are capable**, **you are resilient**, and **you've got this**.

I allow myself to grow
at my own pace,
with kindness and patience.

2

Healing Past Wounds

I want to start this chapter by sharing something deeply personal, something I've held in my heart for a long time. A few years ago, I went through one of the most painful experiences of my life. I remember the night it happened as if it were yesterday. I was sitting on my living room floor with a blanket wrapped around my shoulders, phone in hand, after a conversation that turned my world upside down.

The person I loved deeply—someone I thought would always be there—had just told me that they no longer cared for me the way they used to. In that moment, it felt like my heart shattered into a million little pieces. I felt a mix of shock, betrayal, and an ache so deep I could physically feel it in my chest.

In the days and weeks that followed, I carried that hurt everywhere. I cried in the shower where no one could hear me. I drove aimlessly around town with tears blurring my vision, screaming inside my car because I didn't know what else to do with all that pain. I felt so alone, even when I was surrounded by friends and family.

Have you ever felt that way—like no one else could possibly understand the weight of the hurt you're carrying? That was me. I was hurt and, to be honest, I was also angry. Angry at the person who hurt me, angry at myself for "not being enough," and angry at the universe for letting it all happen.

For a long time, I clung to that pain as if letting it go would mean the hurtful event never mattered. In a strange way, holding onto the hurt felt like holding onto *him*, or at least holding onto the idea of what I thought I had. Pain can be oddly comforting when it's all you have left of someone or something you lost. But that kind of comfort is cold and heavy.

I didn't realize it at first, but carrying that resentment was **only hurting me** further. The person who broke my heart wasn't losing sleep over it—*I* was. It was like I was drinking poison and expecting the other person to suffer. All it did was make me feel worse.

My healing journey began quietly one afternoon, when I found myself scribbling in my journal out of sheer desperation. I poured every ounce of anger, love, sadness, and confusion onto the pages. I wrote letters I never intended to send, just to say all the things I needed to say.

Some days, my writing was just tear-stained pages of questions: *"Why wasn't I enough? How could you do this to me? How do I move forward?"* Other days, it turned into a stream of memories—the good and the bad—that I had been afraid to revisit. And you know what? Little by little, I started to feel a shift inside me. It wasn't an overnight miracle, and I won't pretend it was. But each time I wrote, each time I let a little bit of that emotion out, I felt **just a tiny bit lighter**.

One evening, I decided to do something a bit different—something symbolic. I had written a particularly emotional letter in my journal, one that captured all the pain and anger I'd been carrying. I gently tore that letter out of the journal, read it one last time, and then I took a deep breath and **cut it up** with a pair of scissors.

Snip, snip, snip—I watched that paper turn into dozens of tiny pieces in my hands. With each cut, I imagined I was severing the ties that bound me to that hurt. I was nervous and my hands were shaking, but I also felt this strange sense of *relief*. It was like telling myself, *"Okay, Clara, it's time to let this go now."* Afterward, I threw those tiny paper scraps away. I remember closing my eyes after tossing them out and just sitting there quietly. To my surprise, I didn't feel empty; I felt *free*. I had finally let myself acknowledge the pain, and then I chose to release it. In doing so, I made space inside my heart for something new—peace.

I'm sharing this piece of my story with you because I want you to know that I understand how it feels to be hurt and stuck in that hurt. Past wounds have a way of sneaking into the present, don't they? They can cloud our days and weigh us down, even when we try to outrun them. But I also want you to know that it is possible to heal, to let go, and to find that inner peace you truly deserve. It doesn't mean the past didn't happen or that it doesn't matter. It means that you are no longer allowing it to control your present happiness.

Healing past wounds is one of the hardest—and bravest—things you'll ever do. It takes courage to face the hurt head-on, and even more courage to release it. Sometimes we hold onto pain because we think we have to, or we don't know who we are without it. But you are so much more than the pain you carry, my friend. And letting go of that pain? It isn't about forgetting or saying it was okay. It's about freeing yourself. You deserve to be free.

Your Turn: Reflect and Heal

Now, I want to gently turn the focus to *you*. We all have our own past wounds. Maybe yours comes from a broken relationship like mine did. Or perhaps it's a wound from childhood, or a betrayal by a friend, or a dream you felt was shattered. Whatever it is, it's valid, and so are your feelings about it.

I'd like you to take a deep breath, grab a notebook or a piece of paper, and find a comfortable, quiet space. Let's do a little heart-to-heart reflection. I have a few questions I'd love for you to explore—there's no rush, and there are no right or wrong answers. **This is for your eyes only, so you can be completely honest and gentle with yourself as you write**.

• • •

What is a past wound that still hurts you today? *Describe what happened and, more importantly, how it made you feel. Let it all out on paper—the good, the bad, and the ugly. This is your safe space to acknowledge what hurt you.*

How has holding onto this hurt affected you? *Think about your life since that wound occurred. In what ways do you see that pain showing up? Maybe it makes it hard for you to trust others, or perhaps it's affected your self-esteem or the way you talk to yourself. Be open about the impact it has had on you.*

Is there someone you need to forgive or something you need to let go of? *Sometimes healing involves forgiveness. That might mean forgiving another person, or it might mean forgiving yourself. (Remember, forgiveness isn't about excusing what happened—it's about releasing your burden.) Who or what comes to mind that you might need to release in order to heal?*

What would it look and feel like to finally let this go? *Close your eyes and imagine your life without that heavy hurt in your heart. What would change? How might you change? Would you smile more, sleep better, feel lighter? Paint a picture of the freedom and peace you'd experience if that wound no longer weighed on you.*

Take your time with these questions. You might feel a wave of emotions as you write—that's completely normal. If you need to pause and take a breath or even step away for a moment, do that. This isn't a race; it's a gentle journey. The goal here is to really **understand** what you've been carrying and how it's been affecting you. Awareness is a powerful step toward healing. By writing these thoughts and feelings down, you're acknowledging your pain and giving it a voice. Sometimes, that alone can bring a sense of relief, like a sigh after holding your breath for too long.

The "Cut It Off" Release Ritual

Now that you've spent some time honestly reflecting on your past wound, I want to invite you to join me in a little exercise—a ritual of letting go. This is the same kind of exercise I did with my letter, the one I told you about earlier. I can say from my heart that it was a turning point for me, and I truly hope it will be for you too. Think of this as a symbolic fresh start, a way to tell your heart and mind, *"I'm not going to let this hurt control me anymore."* Even if you're feeling a bit skeptical, I encourage you to give it a try. Sometimes the simple act of doing something physical can help our hearts do something emotional.

When you're ready (and there's no rush—do this whenever it feels right), here's what you can do:

1. **Find a quiet moment.** Set aside a little time for yourself when you won't be interrupted. It could be five minutes or an hour, whatever you can manage. Find a comfortable spot—maybe your bedroom, the couch, or even at your kitchen table with a warm cup of tea. Take a few deep, slow breaths to center yourself. This is your time to focus on healing.

2. **Write down the pain.** On a fresh piece of paper (or a page in a journal or notebook), start writing a letter about the hurt you've been carrying. You might choose to address it to the person who hurt you, to yourself, or just write about the situation—whatever

feels right. Don't worry about punctuation or making it sound nice. Just let your feelings flow onto the page. Say everything you need to say. Cry if you need to. Get angry if you need to. This is your chance to pour it all out. No one else will read this, so be completely honest.

3. **Set your intention to let go.** When you feel like you've written down everything that's bubbling up inside, pause for a moment. Read over what you wrote if you want to (you don't have to if it's too hard). Then, gently place your hand on that page and take a deep breath. As you exhale, say quietly to yourself, *"I am ready to let this go."* You can say it out loud or in your mind, whichever feels more comfortable. The important thing is that you **mean** those words. You are acknowledging that this pain has been a part of you, but you're also telling yourself that it's time to release its hold on you.

4. **Cut it off.** Now for the symbolic part. Grab a pair of scissors (or if you don't have scissors handy, you can tear the paper with your hands). Start cutting that letter or page into pieces. There's no right or wrong way to do this—big pieces, tiny pieces, whatever. As you cut, imagine that each snip of the scissors is cutting a thread that has been tying you to that hurtful past. Visualize those connections snapping and breaking free. You are not destroying a part of yourself or your life; you are destroying the power that pain has had over you. If emotions rise up while you're cutting (and they might), let them come. You might find yourself crying or maybe even laughing a little—it's all okay. Keep going until that paper is in as many pieces as you can manage.

5. **Release and breathe.** Once you have all those little pieces of paper, take them and throw them away. You can toss them in the trash, put them in a recycle bin, or if it's safe and you prefer, you could even burn them in a fireplace or with a candle **(only if you're used to doing that safely!)**. Do whatever feels like a *final goodbye* to those words and all they represent. As you release the pieces, take another deep breath. Inhale slowly, and as you exhale, imagine that heavy weight lifting off your shoulders. Notice how you feel in this moment. Do you sense a bit of relief? Maybe less tension in your body? Even if you still feel sad or a little tender, that's okay—you've begun the process of letting go.

6. **Embrace the new space.** Finally, take a moment to acknowledge what you just did. You faced your pain and took a brave step to release it. That's huge! Sit quietly for a minute and place your hand on your heart. Feel the warmth and strength inside you. You might even say to yourself, *"I am free from this hurt. I am making space for peace."* Visualize that inside your heart or your mind, all that dark, heavy stuff you've been carrying is now cleared out. In its place, see a gentle light or feel a sense of openness. That is the space you've created for healing and inner peace. It might feel unfamiliar at first, but trust that it's a good thing—it's **your** space to fill with self-love, hope, and happiness moving forward.

This ritual is powerful because it gives your mind a clear signal that you are **letting go**. Sometimes our hearts need to see an action to truly believe something. By cutting up that paper, you showed yourself that this pain does not control you any longer. If at any point you still feel the hurt creeping back, remember that healing is not a one-time thing. You can repeat this exercise whenever you need to. Each time, it will reinforce the message that your past does not define you or own you.

Embracing Inner Peace

I want you to take a moment and really feel proud of yourself. What you did wasn't easy. Confronting a past wound and then consciously choosing to release it takes strength—**your** strength. You've proven to yourself that you are capable of facing the hard stuff and taking care of your own heart. That's incredibly powerful.

Now, let's be honest: healing is a journey. You might still think about this hurt from time to time, and that's okay. You might have days when the memories sneak up on you, or moments when you feel a pang of that old pain. Don't be discouraged if that happens. It doesn't mean you failed or that you're back to square one. It just means you're human, and your heart is doing the best it can.

Whenever you feel that hurt resurfacing, remind yourself of what you did today. Remind yourself that you have the courage to acknowledge the pain and the power to let it go. You are not stuck in that past moment anymore; you are here, in the present, actively creating a better, lighter future for yourself.

By letting go of some of that hurt, you've made more room inside for peace and joy. Think of your heart like a garden: you've just pulled out some heavy weeds that were taking up space and blocking the sun. Now there's fresh soil and room for new things to grow—like self-love, confidence, and happiness. You might not see all those new flowers blooming overnight, but trust that they're planted. Every time you choose to release negativity or pain, you water those new seeds of inner peace.

As we continue on this journey through the pages of this journal, know that I'm right here with you, cheering you on every step of the way, like a best friend would. We're in this together, and I am so proud of the progress you're making. **You deserve peace**. **You deserve happiness**. And little by little, step by step, you are claiming it.

Affirmations for Healing & Resilience

Let's finish this chapter with some affirmations—positive statements you can repeat to yourself to encourage healing and build resilience. I like to think of affirmations as **seeds of truth** you plant in your mind. With repetition, they can grow into new, healthier thought patterns. You can say these out loud in the morning, write them on sticky notes and put them on your mirror, or jot them down in your journal daily. Choose the ones that resonate with you (or tweak them to fit your feelings). As you say them, **really absorb the words** and believe them, even if just for that moment.

- *I release the past and embrace peace in the present.*
- *Healing is a journey, and I give myself permission to take it one day at a time.*
- *I am not defined by what hurt me; I am defined by my strength and my heart.*
- *I choose to forgive so that I can set myself free.*
- *My past was only a chapter, not the whole story. I am writing a new chapter of hope and happiness.*
- *I deserve to heal, and I open myself to the love and support around me.*
- *Each day, I grow stronger, wiser, and more at peace.*
- *I lovingly release what I cannot change and focus on what I can create.*

Feel the power in these words as you affirm them. You might even put a hand on your heart when you say them, to physically connect with the emotion. Remember, beautiful friend: **you are healing, you are growing, and you are exactly where you need to be right now.** Every step you take to let go of hurt is a step toward inner peace. And as you continue on this journey, know that Clara *(that's me!)* and countless other women are cheering you on, every step of the way. You are not alone, and you are so worthy of the freedom and happiness that awaits you.

Take a deep breath now—in and out. Feel that hint of lightness in your chest? That's you, healing. That's you, taking back your power from the past. Keep that feeling with you. Whenever you're ready, we'll turn the page and continue this beautiful journey of growth together.

3

The Present Moment

I remember a couple of years ago, sitting on the warm sand at Newport Beach with an orange sunset painting the sky. It should have been a perfect moment. But even with the waves gently rolling in and the salty ocean breeze on my face, I realized I wasn't *really* there. My body was watching the sunset, but my mind was somewhere else entirely. I was replaying an old fight I'd had with a close friend and at the same time worrying about a big project deadline coming up at work. My heart felt heavy, and I was missing the beauty right in front of me because I was stuck in my head.

As I sat there lost in thought, a little part of me noticed how much I was missing. *How many times had I done this?* How often had I been physically present but mentally a million miles away? I felt a pang of guilt and sadness thinking about all the small joys I might have overlooked because I was either rehashing yesterday's problems or stressing about tomorrow's uncertainties. In that moment, with the sky turning pink and gold, I made a gentle promise to myself: *I deserve to fully experience moments like this.* We all do.

Letting Go of Yesterday and Tomorrow

Being present is **hard**, especially when our minds love to hang onto the past or leap into the future. Trust me, I've been there. On that beach day, I finally acknowledged how much I was carrying with me that was pulling me out of the now. The worries, the regrets, the what-ifs—they were like heavy anchors tied to my heart. No wonder I felt weighed down and distracted! I realized I needed to let some things go if I wanted to feel lighter and truly live in the present.

Write it down honestly. Sometimes just seeing it on paper is the first step to letting it go. I know it might feel a bit vulnerable to do this, but remember, I'm right here with you like a friend holding your hand. It's okay —this is for your eyes only, and there's no judgment at all.

But first, let's gently figure out what your anchors might be. Take a moment to think about what's been occupying your mind lately. Is it an old memory that still stings, or maybe a worry that keeps you up at night?

...

When was the last time you remember feeling truly present?

What were you doing, and what did that moment feel like for you?

The "Cut It Off" Ritual

What is one thought, worry, or memory that has been weighing on you or pulling you out of the present moment? Describe it.

Now that you've identified something you want to release, let's proceed with our ritual. Grab a piece of paper and answer the question above. Make sure you have the words or a symbol of that worry or memory on the paper in front of you.

1. **Take a moment:** Pause and really look at what you wrote. Acknowledge the feelings it brings up. You can even say out loud, *"This has been weighing on me."* It's important to recognize it one last time before we let it go.

2. **Cut it up:** Take a pair of scissors *(carefully!)* and start cutting that paper into small pieces. As you cut, imagine you are cutting the ties that this thought has around you. I sometimes like to say, *"I'm cutting you off now. You don't get to control me anymore."* It might feel a little silly, but trust me, it feels empowering.

3. **Dispose of the pieces:** Once you've snipped that paper into confetti, decide what you want to do with the scraps. You can toss them in the trash as a sign that this worry belongs in the waste now, not in your mind. Or you could even flush them or bury them in the ground if that feels meaningful to you. Do whatever resonates with you, safely.

4. **Take a deep breath:** After you've physically cut and thrown away that worry, close your eyes and take a slow, deep breath. Inhale the new freedom, exhale the old stress. You might place a hand on your heart or even give yourself a little hug. Notice how you feel in this moment. Maybe lighter, maybe a bit unsure—however you feel is completely okay.

This ritual is a physical way to say *I'm done carrying this for now.* When I did it, I remember feeling a mix of relief and disbelief. Relief because it felt good to do something tangible to release my worry, and disbelief because part of me never thought I could actually let it go. But guess what? I did, and it was the start of me finding more peace in everyday life.

• • •

How did it feel to cut up and dispose of that piece of paper? Did you experience any relief, resistance, sadness, or something else during this ritual? Write about anything you noticed.

It's okay if you still feel a little attached to what you wrote — letting go can be a process. You might even try this ritual again for other things, or repeat it if that thought creeps back. Each time, it can get a bit easier.

Guided Mindfulness Exercise: Coming Back to Now

After letting go of something that's been distracting you, it's helpful to fill that space with a gentle return to the present. One of the best ways I've found to do that is through a short mindfulness exercise. Don't worry, this isn't going to be a long, formal meditation or anything *(unless you want it to be!)*. It's just a simple practice you and I can do right here, right now, to center ourselves.

Think of it like this: now that we've symbolically cut off a weight from the past or future, let's anchor ourselves in *this moment*, where life is actually happening. We can do it together. Ready?

1. Get comfortable: Find a cozy spot to sit or lie down. You can close your eyes if you feel safe doing so, or simply soften your gaze toward the floor. Imagine I'm sitting next to you, doing the same thing—you're not doing this alone.

2. Take a few deep breaths: Inhale slowly through your nose, let your belly fill with air, then exhale gently through your mouth. Do this a few times. With each exhale, feel your shoulders relax, as if you are physically releasing any leftover tension.

3. Notice your surroundings: Now, pay attention to the sensations around you. What do you hear? Maybe the hum of the fridge, the rustle of trees outside, or just calm silence. What do you feel? Notice the texture of the chair or floor supporting you, and the temperature of the air on your skin. You don't have to judge any of it as good or bad—just notice it. This is you being present.

4. Mind your thoughts: If a thought pops into your head *(and it probably will, that's okay!)*, see if you can just watch it float by like a cloud in the sky. You might gently say to yourself, "Hey thought, I'll get back to you later." Then bring your focus back to your breath or to the sounds and sensations around you. There's no need to fight your thoughts or feel bad when they come. Just guide your attention back to the now, as kindly as you would guide a friend.

5. Stay for a moment: Continue this gentle noticing for about one minute, or as long as feels comfortable. You can set a timer for a minute if you like, or just take about 5-10 slow breaths. There's no rush. Simply be there, experiencing each moment as it comes.

6. Return slowly: When you're ready, take one more deep breath and slowly open your eyes (if they were closed). Look around and bring your awareness back to your surroundings. Notice that the world is still here—and you are a part of it, awake in this moment.

How do you feel now? Even if you feel just 1% more calm or present than before, that's a win. When I first tried this, I was amazed at how much I noticed in just one minute of really tuning in. I heard birds outside that I hadn't paid attention to before, and I felt my own heartbeat slowing down. I felt more *here* than I had in a long time, and it only took sixty seconds of mindfulness.

• • •

Take a moment to write about your experience with that short mindfulness exercise. How did it feel to focus on the present moment? What did you notice around you or within you?

Remember, there's no "right" way to feel. Your experience is uniquely yours. You might have felt peaceful, or your mind might have wandered a dozen times. Whatever happened is okay. The fact that you gave it a try is something to be proud of!

Embracing the Here and Now

Being present is called a "practice" for a reason—it takes practice! Just like building a muscle, every time you bring your attention back to *now*, you're strengthening your ability to live in the moment. And the more you do it, the more natural it will become.

I want to share something personal: these days, I still catch my mind drifting to old worries or racing toward future plans *(I'm only human, after all!)*. But now I have tools to gently guide myself back. Sometimes it's as simple as taking a deep breath and noticing the sun on my face, or reminding myself that *right now, in this very moment, I'm okay*. Other times, if I'm really stuck on something, I'll do the "cut it off" ritual again or call a close friend to talk it out.

What matters is that you find what helps you come back to the present. Maybe it's a mindfulness breathing exercise like we just practiced. Maybe it's journaling out your feelings each morning to clear your head. Or maybe it's stepping outside for a five-minute break to feel the fresh air on your skin. Find the little rituals that bring you home to yourself.

• • •

What is one small action or habit you can commit to in your daily life to help you stay more mindful and present? It could be putting your phone away during meals, pausing to stretch and breathe every couple of hours, or keeping a gratitude list. Write down one idea and why it speaks to you.

I truly hope you feel proud of yourself—because I'm proud of you. You've taken a brave step in not only identifying something that's been weighing you down, but also actively working to let it go and cultivate presence—that's huge! As your friend, I'm cheering you on every step of the way. Every moment you catch yourself and return to now is a little victory. Life is happening in these tiny moments, and you deserve to fully live them.

Affirmations for Presence & Clarity

Before we wrap up this chapter, I want to leave you with some heart-warming affirmations. Think of these as little *mantras* or phrases you can say to yourself to reinforce that sense of presence and clear-mindedness. I like to jot my favorites on sticky notes or say them in the mirror in the morning *(feels goofy at first, but it sets a positive tone)*. As you read these, imagine me, your friend Clara, saying them to you—because I believe every word, and I believe in *you*:

- *I am here, I am present, and this moment is enough.*
- *I deserve to slow down and savor life's little moments.*
- *I release the past and the future; I choose to find peace in the now.*
- *With each breath, I anchor myself to the present.*
- *I am allowed to take things one step at a time.*
- *Clarity and calm are available to me in this very moment.*
- *I am grounded, I am centered, and I trust myself in the here and now.*

Feel free to add your own spin to these or create new ones that resonate with you. The key is that they should make you feel comforted and empowered. Say them silently or out loud *(I often whisper mine under my breath when I need a quick reset)*.

I hope you're feeling a big warm hug from these pages, because I'm genuinely rooting for you. Practicing mindfulness and staying present is one of the greatest gifts you can give yourself. It's a way of saying, *"My life matters, this moment matters."* And it does—*you* matter.

As you go forward, remember that it's okay to stumble and forget and then remember again to come back to now. I still have to remind myself daily! But with practice, it gets easier and more natural, like coming home to a place of peace inside you.

So take it day by day, moment by moment. And remember, I'm right here with you, learning and growing alongside you. Let's keep embracing the present together, one breath at a time.

My life unfolds beautifully when I slow down and pay attention.

4

Healthy Boundaries

Well, hello there, you! Today, I want to chat about something very personal and incredibly empowering: **boundaries**. You know, those sometimes-tough, sometimes-scary lines we draw to protect our energy and personal space. Grab a cozy blanket or a cup of tea, and let's settle in. This chapter is all about learning to confidently say, *"This is my space, and I deserve to keep it safe."* Trust me, by the end of this, it'll feel like you're having a heart-to-heart with your best friend *(that's me, Clara!)* about how to guard your precious energy. Ready? Let's do this together.

Learning to Say "No" (The Hard Way)

I want to start by sharing a story of mine—one I haven't told many people. If you know a bit about me, you might know I grew up in sunny, picture-perfect Newport Beach. Think ocean breezes and fancy yachts, and a world where everyone smiled and said, *"I'm fine, thank you,"* even when they weren't. In my family, I was the *"good girl"*: always polite, always accommodating. I had every material comfort, yet I often felt a heavy pressure to make everyone happy. And oh boy, did that pressure follow me into adulthood.

In my twenties, I had a close friend ***(let's call her Megan)***. Megan was fun and big-hearted, but she didn't really understand **boundaries**. She would call me at all hours to vent about her boyfriend drama, or she'd *"volunteer"* me to help her with projects *without* asking. And me? I always said yes.

I remember one Friday night—exhausted after a long work week—I had planned a much-needed cozy evening solo. Pajamas, face mask, a good book... the whole self-care package. Just as I lit a candle and exhaled, my phone buzzed. It was Megan, in tears over yet another fight with her boyfriend, begging me to come over. Every part of me wanted to say, *"I'm sorry, I can't tonight."* But my mouth? It automatically said, *"Of course, I'll be right there."*

So off I went, driving across town late at night and comforting her until 3 AM. By the time I got home, I was beyond drained. I crawled into bed feeling resentful and even a little angry. Not at Megan—at **myself!** Why was it so hard for me to just say no? I stared at the ceiling, realizing this wasn't a one-time thing. It kept happening. I'd sacrifice my own needs to cater to others. I was the queen of people-pleasing, and it was slowly crushing my spirit.

The breaking point came a few months later. I had agreed to help organize a charity event *(because of course I had said "yes" to that too)*. It ate up all my free time. One night, while juggling phone calls for the event and work emails (and yet another distraught call from Megan), I just **broke down**. I remember sinking to the bathroom floor, sobbing. I felt pulled in a million directions and completely empty. In that teary moment, a thought bubbled up that changed my life: *I can't live like this. Something has to change. I have to change.*

That was the night I decided to start setting boundaries. Scary? Oh, absolutely. Necessary? More than anything. The very next day, with my heart pounding, I called Megan. Gently, I told her how much I cared about her, but that I couldn't be her 24/7 on-call therapist anymore. I suggested she consider talking to a professional, or at least that we plan our calls for earlier in the evening. My voice shook—I was *so* nervous. Her initial reaction? She was hurt and confused. *"I thought best friends are always there for each other,"* she said. Ouch—that stabbed me in the heart. For a second I wanted to take it all back and apologize profusely. But I held firm (while silently freaking out inside). I explained that I do love her, and that being there for each other also means respecting each other's needs.

To my surprise, after a day or two, Megan called and apologized to me. She admitted she'd been leaning on me too much and hadn't realized it. Can you imagine my relief? I practically melted with gratitude. Now, not every boundary I've set has been received this well, but that first experience taught me something crucial: the people who truly care about you will respect your boundaries. And those who don't? Well, they might not be the right people to keep in your inner circle.

Growing up in Newport Beach's world of *"yes, of course"* and polite smiles, I used to think setting boundaries was selfish. I worried people would think I was mean, or that I didn't care about them. But here's what I learned through that experience (and many that followed): **setting healthy boundaries is one of the most loving things you can do**—for yourself and for others. It's not about pushing people away; it's about protecting your own heart and energy so you can show up as the best, healthiest version of you. After that turning point, I started saying "no" when I really couldn't take something on. And guess what? The world didn't end! Instead, I felt lighter, more respected, and more in control of my life than ever before.

Understanding Boundaries: Self-Love in Action

Let's talk a bit about what boundaries actually are, because for the longest time, I had no clue. I used to picture boundaries as these cold, hard walls—imagine a giant stone fortress around my heart *(dramatic, I know!)*. But I've since realized that healthy boundaries are more like a warm, fuzzy blanket around your personal space. They keep you feeling safe and comfortable. They're not about shutting people out; they're about teaching people how to love and respect you better.

Think of it this way: *you* are a beautiful garden. Your energy, your time, your feelings—those are your flowers, your sunshine, your soil. Now, what does every beautiful garden need? A little fence or border, right? Not to isolate it, but to protect it from being trampled. **Boundaries are the fence around your garden.** They say, *"Hey, this is my special space. You're welcome to enjoy it with me, but please don't walk all over it."* Without that fence, well... people (or the critters of life) might wander in and crush your flowers without even realizing it.

I had to learn that saying "no" or standing up for myself didn't make me a bad friend, daughter, or partner. It made me an honest one. It made me a **healthy** one. When I finally got it through my head that my needs matter too, it was like a lightbulb turned on. Setting boundaries is truly self-love in action. It's you telling yourself *and* the world: *"I value me. I value my time, my energy, my feelings. And I'm going to protect them."*

For so long, I believed that if I set a boundary, I would let people down or maybe they'd even leave me. But here's the truth (and I say this with so much love): the people who belong in your life *want* you to take care of yourself. They'll understand when you say, "I can't make it tonight," or "Please don't joke about that, it hurts my feelings," or "I need an hour to myself after work." In fact, being open about your needs might even inspire them to respect their own boundaries, too. And the people who kick up a fuss, who guilt-trip you, or call you selfish? I know it stings, but those might be the people you need to step back from. (Tough medicine, I know. I've been there and **ouch**... it hurt. But in the long run, it was so worth it.)

Once I started setting a few boundaries, something almost magical happened: I had energy again! I wasn't constantly running on empty, because I wasn't giving, giving, giving to everyone else with nothing left for myself. I had time to actually breathe—to do yoga in the mornings, to read a book without interruption, even to meet new people who respected the fact that I have a life of my own. I became a lot less resentful, too. Instead of secretly seething when someone took advantage of my kindness, I began to be upfront about what I could or couldn't do. It felt **so** weird at first *(I won't lie)*. The first few times I said, "No, I can't babysit your dog this weekend—I need some rest," I basically had to pep-talk myself before *and* after. But each time, it got a little bit easier. And each time, I respected myself more.

Here's something I want you to remember, as your friend who cares deeply about you: **You deserve the same love and care that you so freely give to others.** Setting boundaries is loving yourself. It's like giving Future You a big hug and saying, *"I got you—we're going to be okay."* It might feel uncomfortable at first (even downright scary), but with practice, it becomes empowering. It becomes second nature. And it will change your life in the most beautiful ways—I *pinky promise.* 🤞

Reflection & Journaling Prompts: Your Boundaries, Your Truth

Now, let's gently turn the spotlight onto **you**. Don't worry, this isn't a test or homework—think of it as your best friend *(me!)* casually asking you some questions over coffee that might make you go, *"Hmm, I never thought about that."* There are no right or wrong answers here. This is your safe space to explore what boundaries mean for you, and where you might need a little boundary boost in your life. Grab your pen and let your thoughts flow onto the page. Take your time with these prompts, and be extra kind to yourself as you answer them:

...

Think of a time when you felt completely drained or taken advantage of by someone (even if they didn't mean to). What happened, and how did it make you feel? What do you wish you could have said or done in that situation to protect your energy?

What is one area of your life–be it work, friendship, family, dating, etc.–where you struggle to set boundaries? Why do you think setting boundaries there is so tough for you? Write down any fears or beliefs that come up (for example, "I worry they won't like me," or "I was taught that family comes first, no matter what").

Describe how your body or mind lets you know when a boundary has been crossed. Do you get a knot in your stomach? A headache? Do you feel anxious or maybe resentful? Write about those feelings and physical clues. Think of it like your inner self whispering, "Something's not right here," when your boundary is breached.

Envision a current situation where you feel stretched thin or uncomfortable because your boundaries aren't as strong as they could be. Now imagine yourself setting a clear boundary in that situation. What would you say or do differently? How might the other person ideally react, and how would you feel afterward?

Identify one small boundary you can experiment with this week. It could be as simple as taking **30** *minutes of "me time" with no interruptions, not answering work emails after a certain hour, or politely declining a favor you really don't have time for. How do you imagine you'll feel after doing this? Excited? Nervous? Relieved?* Write it down.

Take a deep breath. That last question—that small boundary you plan to try—hold it close to your heart. You don't have to act on it this very second, but commit to giving it a try soon. And remember, I'm right here cheering you on. Every "no" or "not this time" that honors your needs is a huge **YES** to your own well-being.

(Take a moment to finish writing your thoughts. I'll wait...)

Great job! I know these reflections might stir up some feelings—maybe a mix of empowerment and a little fear. That's okay. Change often feels that way at first. Keep in mind, boundaries are a skill, and like any skill, you get better with practice. Be gentle with yourself, just as I'm being gentle with you.

The "Cut It Off": Releasing Unhealthy Boundaries

Alright, now for something a little different *(and trust me, it's both meaningful and kinda fun!)*. By now you're familiar with our **"Cut It Off"** ritual, and we're going to use it again—this time to release those weak or unhealthy boundaries that are no longer serving you. Since you've done this before, I'll keep the instructions brief. Let's do a quick refresher:

What you'll need: A piece of paper, a pen, and a pair of scissors. (If you don't have scissors handy, tearing the paper works too!)

Quick Steps for the "Cut It Off" Ritual:

1. **Name it:** Think of one boundary struggle that's been draining you or holding you back. Maybe it's a person who constantly pushes past your comfort zone, or an old habit of yours like always saying "yes" when you want to say "no." Write down a word or sentence on your paper that represents this boundary issue.

2. **Declare your release:** Now, write a simple statement declaring that you're ready to let this go. It could be something like, *"I release this pattern,"* or *"I cut off this guilt I feel."* Whatever words feel right—this is you telling yourself that you're ready to be free of this.

3. **Cut it off:** Grab your scissors (or use your hands to rip) and **cut that paper into pieces.** You can snip it into strips or tear it up—do whatever feels good. As you cut, imagine that you are literally cutting away the ties of this old boundary issue. Picture those unhealthy boundary feelings getting smaller with each cut.

4. **Discard and breathe:** Once you've cut it into lots of pieces, go ahead and throw those pieces away. *(If it feels right and you can do so safely, you could even burn them in a fireplace or sink—just be careful!)*. As you dispose of the paper, take a long, deep breath in... then exhale slowly. As you breathe out, imagine the weight of that boundary issue **whooshing** out of you. Feel that lightness? That's you letting go.

5. **Affirm your freedom:** To finish our ritual, say something kind and empowering to yourself. Maybe quietly or out loud (your choice!). You could say, *"I am free from this now,"* or *"I deserve to feel safe*

and respected." If you feel like it, do a little victory shake or happy dance to literally *shake* off the old energy. *(Yes, I totally do a goofy happy dance in my living room after these releases—no shame, it feels great!)*

How did that feel? If you're a little teary or emotional, that's completely okay. I often cry when I do these kinds of releases—it's emotional because you're standing up for yourself in a way you maybe never have before. And if you felt a bit **silly** doing it, that's okay too! I remember giggling the first time I tried something like this, wondering, *"Is this really going to help?"* But it *did* help. There's something powerful about physically cutting those ties and letting go. It's like telling your mind and body, *"Hey, we're really doing this—we're moving on."*

• • •

Feel free to write down any feelings or thoughts that came up during this exercise. This is your space to process.

You did a wonderful job. I'm giving you a huge virtual high-five right now! 🖐️🎉 You just took another big step in claiming your space and protecting your well-being.

Visualize Your Boundaries: The Personal Bubble Exercise

Now that you've symbolically snipped away the old, let's create something new and positive. This next part is a bit creative and very empowering. It's time to **visualize** your boundaries in a way that feels uplifting *(and maybe even a little fun!)*. I'm a very visual person, and this exercise helped me tons—I hope it helps you, too.

I like to call this the **Personal Bubble Visualization**. Don't worry if you're not "artistic"—this isn't about making a pretty drawing. It's about creating something meaningful for *you*. Here's how to do it:

- **Imagine your safe space:** Close your eyes for a moment and picture yourself surrounded by a protective bubble or shield. It can look however you want. Maybe it's a shimmering gold light encircling you. Maybe it's a cool purple force field, like you're a superhero (because hello, *you are* a bit of a superhero now with these new boundary-setting powers!). I often imagine a warm, rosy glow around my body, like I'm in my own little world where only good vibes can enter. Take a few deep breaths and really see this bubble in your mind's eye. This is your boundary - warm, loving, and **yours**.

- **Draw or de—ibe it:** Open your eyes and grab some colorful pens. Now, either **draw** your personal boundary bubble on the second page following or, if drawing isn't your jam, **describe it in words**. You might sketch a simple figure of you with a circle around it representing your bubble. Maybe add some cute stars or hearts on that bubble to show it's positive and loving. Or write a description: *"My boundary is like an energy field—it's soft and kind, but it keeps out negativity or disrespect."* Be as imaginative as you like. If you want to draw a castle with a moat and dragons guarding it because that's how secure you want to feel, do it! If you prefer a modern twist and imagine a high-tech laser shield, go for it. This is **your vision.**

- **Place what matters inside:** On your drawing (or in your written description), highlight what's **inside** your boundary with you. What do you cherish and want to keep within your protected space? For example, inside my bubble I wrote words like "self-respect," "peace," "family," "true friends," "creative energy," and "joy." These are the things (and people and values) I allow in my space because they nourish me. Think about what you want to allow into your personal space. Who and what makes you feel safe, loved, and energized? Write their names or draw little symbols for them inside your boundary circle.

- **Mark what stays out:** Now consider what you're keeping **outside** with your healthy boundary. This could be negative self-talk, toxic relationships, overwork, guilt—anything you're ready to say "no more" to. Write those things *around* the *outside* of your boundary drawing (you can add a little "**✕**" or a stop-sign symbol next to each to show they're not allowed in). On mine, I wrote things like "constant guilt," "people who don't respect 'no'," and "saying yes when I mean no." It felt so good to see those on the outside of my bubble, far away from me. Go ahead and mark whatever you want to keep out: maybe "unnecessary drama," "exhaustion," "being taken for granted," etc.

- Reflect on your picture: Take a look at what you created. That's your boundary, visually mapped out. Doesn't it feel more real now? I bet it looks pretty amazing, because it's a reflection of you taking care of yourself. If you ever feel your resolve wavering, come back to this page. You can even close your eyes and summon that bubble or shield around you whenever you need a quick reminder that you are protected. (Personally, I sometimes take a quick "bubble breath": I'll inhale and imagine drawing my bubble around me, then exhale and see it shining. It centers me—especially before a tough conversation or when I'm about to say no to someone.)

This creative visualization is a tool for your mind and soul. It's like a little promise to yourself: "I will keep what's precious inside, and keep out what harms me." And guess what? You deserve to feel safe. You deserve a life where you get to choose where your energy goes. Keep this drawing or description as a reminder that you have an invisible bubble of love and self-respect around you all the time.

Self-Care Strategies: Keeping Your Boundaries Strong (Bestie to Bestie)

You've done some amazing work so far—reflecting, releasing, visualizing. Now let's talk about how to **maintain** those healthy boundaries in everyday life. Think of this as me, your bestie, giving you my top tips while we lounge on the couch in our PJs. These are strategies that have helped me keep my boundaries strong *(even when life tries to test them, as it inevitably will!)*. You got this, and I'm right here cheering you on:

- **Start small and be consistent:** If you're new to boundaries, it's totally okay (even wise) to start with small changes. Maybe begin by setting a tiny boundary with your time: for example, no phone calls after 9 PM because that's your wind-down time, or taking a short walk alone every Sunday as your personal recharge ritual. Small, consistent boundaries will build your "confidence muscle." Each time you follow through on a boundary, you'll trust yourself more—and others will too.

- **Practice saying "no" (it gets easier!):** I know, I know—saying "no" can feel like the hardest thing in the world when you're used to saying "yes." One trick that helped me was having a few polite but firm phrases ready to go. Try saying, *"I'm sorry, I won't be able to make it,"* or *"I have other plans,"* (even if that plan is literally to relax at home—that *is* a valid plan!). You don't have to give a detailed excuse; a simple "I can't this time, but thank you for thinking of me" is enough. If you're not used to this, you can even practice in the mirror or jot down a little script in your journal. It might feel awkward at first, but it's so empowering once you get the hang of it.

- **Set digital boundaries:** In our always-connected world, your phone can feel like an open door to anyone at any time. It's okay to set boundaries with technology, too. For instance, you might decide not to reply to work emails after dinner, or let friends know you won't be checking texts during your study time or workouts. I started leaving my phone in another room when I sleep so I'm not tempted to respond to late-night messages. And guess what? The world kept spinning, and I slept a lot better. Give yourself permission to unplug without guilt.

- **Use gentle reminders for others:** Sometimes even the people who love us might forget or unknowingly push a boundary. It's perfectly fine to remind them—gently. If a friend keeps interrupting your quiet time by calling, you can say, *"I love talking to you. Can we plan our calls, or could you text me first to see if I'm free? I've been needing more quiet time lately."* You're not offending them; you're letting them know how to love you better. Real friends will get it, and they'll appreciate knowing how to support you.

- **Check in with yourself regularly:** Make it a habit to pause every so often and ask, *"How am I feeling about the balance in my life? Am I giving too much anywhere? Do I need to reinforce a boundary?"* I do this kind of self check-in about once a week *(usually Sunday evenings with a cup of herbal tea in hand)*. If I notice I'm feeling drained or resentful about something, it's usually a sign I need to adjust or reinforce a boundary. Think of it like tending that garden we talked about—pulling out the weeds *(things that don't serve you)* and watering the flowers *(things that do)*.

- **Celebrate and recharge:** Every time you honor a boundary, celebrate it! Seriously, give yourself a mental high-five or treat yourself to something nice. Maybe after you *(finally!)* tell your cousin you can't babysit for the third weekend in a row because you need some **you time**, you celebrate by taking a luxurious bubble bath or watching your favorite show with zero guilt. Positive reinforcement isn't just for puppies—we humans thrive on it too. Rewarding yourself for taking care of yourself will encourage you to keep it up.

- **Have a boundary buddy:** If you can, find a friend or someone you trust who also wants to work on boundaries, and support each other. You can share experiences, pump each other up before a tough conversation, and debrief afterward. I had a *"boundary buddy,"* my friend Alexis, and we'd literally text each other things like, *"I said no to my boss about working late. It was scary, but I did it!"* and the other would reply with all the celebratory emojis. 🎉 It made the whole process feel less lonely and more like a team effort.

Remember, maintaining boundaries is an **ongoing practice**. Even now, I have moments where I slip up—maybe I let someone cross a line, or I overcommit myself and start feeling that old familiar burnout. When that happens, I try not to beat myself up. I recognize it, then course-correct. Self-care is a journey, not a destination, and each day is a new chance to honor yourself. And I'm right here, proud of every step you're taking.

Affirmations for Boundaries & Self-Respect

I want to leave you with one of my favorite tools for reinforcing all this good work: **affirmations**. Think of affirmations as little love notes to your soul—powerful, positive statements that remind you of the strong, self-respecting, boundary-setting queen you truly are. You can say these to yourself in the mirror each morning, write them on sticky notes and put them around your space, or jot them in your journal. They might feel a bit cheesy or awkward at first *(I definitely felt super weird talking to myself in the mirror initially!)*, but trust me: the more you repeat them, the more you start to internalize the truth of the words.

Here are some empowering mantras to help you stand tall in your boundaries and nurture that self-respect we've been building:

- *I deserve to protect my time, energy, and personal space.*
- *Saying "no" when I need to is an act of self-care, not selfishness.*
- *I am worthy of relationships that respect and honor my boundaries.*
- *It's okay to prioritize myself—I can't pour from an empty cup.*
- *My feelings and needs are valid, and I have the right to express them.*
- *Each time I set a healthy boundary, I grow stronger and more authentic.*
- *I let go of guilt and embrace the freedom that comes from speaking up for what I need.*
- *Protecting my energy allows me to show up as my best self.*

Read those again, slowly. Maybe even pick one or two that really resonate with you and say them out loud **right now**. Notice how you feel when you say these words. Even if you feel a bit shy or doubtful, that's okay. Keep at it. Over time, these affirmations will plant little seeds in your mind that grow into a solid belief: the belief that you *matter*. Because you absolutely do. (You **so, so** do.)

Big hugs, my treasured soul. 🤗 Setting boundaries is brave work—it's heart-work. It's you choosing to love yourself a little more each day. I hope my stories, tips, and exercises in this chapter made you feel understood, supported, and above all, **empowered** to protect your energy and personal space.

Remember, I'm walking this journey with you. I've stumbled and learned, and I'm still learning. We're in this together. Whenever you need a reminder of your strength, come back to these pages. Hear my voice cheering you on: *"You've got this. You're doing great. Keep honoring yourself, beautiful."*

Now take a nice deep breath, smile *(even just a tiny smile counts)*, and say it with me: *"My space and energy are precious, and I am allowed to protect them."*

On to the next chapter—stronger and more self-loving than ever. **I'm so proud of you!**

5

Creativity and Expression

Hello, my beautiful friend. I want to start this chapter by wrapping you in a big, warm hug because we're about to dive into something really close to my heart: creativity and self-expression. Think of this chapter as our cozy coffee chat about letting our inner colors shine. I'll share a bit of my own journey, and I promise to keep it completely real. We'll explore why creativity isn't just for **"artists"** in studios—it's for everyone, including you and me, right here in our everyday lives. By the end, we'll have some gentle journaling prompts, a fun little exercise to shake off self-doubt, and a bundle of loving affirmations to remind you how wonderfully creative you truly are. Ready? Let's go!

My Journey to Freeing My Creativity

From the outside, my childhood might have looked like a picture-perfect postcard. But on the inside, little Clara was wrestling with a secret fear. See, I always adored creative things—doodling silly cartoons in my notebook, making up dramatic songs about my dog, and choreographing ridiculous dance moves in front of my mirror. To me, these little acts of creativity felt magical. They were my way of expressing all the goofy, glittery feelings bouncing around in my heart.

However, growing up in an environment where everything seemed flawless, I started to worry that I wasn't. At school, I remember painting a sunset with every color in the crayon box—I was so proud of that messy rainbow sky! But one of my classmates *(let's call her Miss Perfect Painter)* smirked and said, *"Sunsets aren't blue and purple like that."* In that moment, I felt my cheeks burn with embarrassment, and a tiny thought crept in: *maybe I'm not an artist... maybe I'm just being silly.* That little comment planted a seed of self-doubt that I carried for years.

Fast forward to grown-up Clara, and I still had that creative spark inside me—but it was buried under layers of fear and perfectionism. In college and my early twenties, I chose "safe" hobbies that I thought were more acceptable. Instead of singing my heart out or painting, I focused on academic stuff and things I knew I could excel in. Don't get me wrong, I learned a lot, but a part of me felt like a wild, colorful bird trapped in a cage. I was afraid to draw or dance just for fun because I might "do it wrong." Can you imagine? Doing **fun** wrong? It sounds crazy, but that's truly how I felt. I had convinced myself that if I couldn't be the best, I shouldn't do it at all.

Then life, as it often does, gave me a wake-up call. A few years ago, when I went through a really tough breakup. It was the kind that turns your world upside down and inside out. I felt lost, and my heart was heavy with emotions I didn't know how to handle. One night, curled up on my couch with tear-stained cheeks, I felt an overwhelming urge to grab a journal and just scribble. I wrote words, I drew angry jagged lines and sad little faces, I splashed colors across the page with absolutely zero plan. It was raw and messy and... incredibly freeing. For the first time in ages, I wasn't creating something to impress anyone or to be "good" at it. I was just letting my feelings flow. By the time I put down that pen, something had shifted inside me. I had found a little piece of myself again, hiding in those doodles and ramblings.

That experience was a turning point. I realized creativity wasn't about making something perfect—it was about expressing my soul and healing my heart. I started allowing myself to explore again, like when I was that goofy kid singing about my dog. I took up gardening and planted the craziest, most colorful flowers. I joined a casual weekend art class where splattering paint was encouraged *(so much fun!)*, and yes, I even danced in my living room to '90s pop like nobody was watching. Each time I let go and created with joy rather than judgment, I felt more alive. Creativity became my therapy, my best friend, and a path back to myself.

So, that's my story in a nutshell: a girl who had to unlearn *perfection* to find her real, messy, wonderful creative self. And guess what? If I can do it, so can you. No matter where you come from or what others have told you —you have this vibrant creative spirit inside just waiting to bloom. Let's explore it together, okay?

Creativity Lives in Everyone (Yes, Even You!)

There's a big, fat myth out there that "creativity" is only for professional artists, painters, writers—you know, the ones with fancy studios or published Books. But *pssst*, lean in, I'm going to tell you a secret: **Creativity lives in EVERY single one of us.** It's true! You, me, the barista who made your coffee, your grandma, your best friend—we all have that spark. Creativity isn't just about painting a masterpiece or writing a novel. It's also in the way you cooked your special spaghetti recipe last week, adding a dash of cinnamon just because. It's in how you stacked those pillows on your couch with a unique flair, or how you told a funny story that made your friend laugh until she snorted tea out of her nose *(oops! Been there!)*. Every time you think outside the box, solve a problem in your own way, or express yourself from the heart – **that's creativity, love.**

The thing is, as kids, we were—I naturally creative. Remember finger painting without a care in the world? Or making up wild stories about unicorns on the playground? As children, we didn't judge our creativity; we just played. But as we grow up, many of us start to doubt ourselves. Maybe someone told you you're "not the creative type," or you began comparing yourself to others *(ugh, comparison—the ultimate joy-killer)*. Maybe you think, *"I can barely draw a stick figure,"* or *"I'm not talented enough to be creative."* I hear you, because I've been in that headspace too. But let me gently and lovingly call BS on that.

Being creative **doesn't** mean being perfect. It doesn't mean you have to sell your art on Etsy or get a million likes on your doodle. Creativity is a form of self-expression, and it's already inside you, waiting for you to give it a little attention. It's like a friendly little puppy tugging at your shoelaces, saying, *"Hey, let's play!"* You wouldn't ignore a cute puppy, would you? Of course not! So, let's not ignore the playful, creative you either.

In truth, creativity is so much more than art projects. It's also how we adapt to life's changes and solve problems. When you're figuring out how to budget your money till the end of the month and you create a fun challenge out of making pantry meals, that's creativity. When you find a new shortcut to get to work on time, that's creativity. When you cheer up a sad friend with a made-up goofy poem, oh boy, that's creativity and kindness rolled into one.

So let's embrace this fact: **you are a creative soul.** It doesn't matter if your doodles look like amorphous blobs or if the only thing you've drawn in years is a smiley face in a foggy mirror. What matters is that you have a voice and a heart that deserve to express themselves. Creativity is your birthright, my friend. It's part of being human, part of being you. Let's claim it and set it free, one gentle step at a time.

Let's Reflect: Getting to Know Your Creative Side

Alright, love, now that we've established you **do** have a creative spark *(no denying it, I see that twinkle in your eyes!)*, let's do a little exploring. Grab the colorful pens you have, and let's reflect together.

Don't worry—these are not tests or homework. Think of them as our heart-to-heart prompts, like I'm right there beside you, legs curled up on the couch, asking you these questions with a soft smile. Write whatever comes to mind; there are no wrong answers here, promise!

• • •

Back to Childhood Joy: What's one creative thing you loved doing as a child? *Did you build epic blanket forts, draw on the sidewalk with chalk, or make up silly dances to your favorite song? How did it make you feel back then?*

Everyday Creativity: In what tiny ways are you already creative in your daily life? Think about the meals you cook, the jokes you tell, how you style your hair or mix and match your clothes. List a few things—you might surprise yourself by how creative you already are!

The Comparison Monster: Have you ever held back from a creative activity you wanted to try because you felt you weren't "good enough," or you were comparing yourself to someone else? (It's okay, we all have.) What did that little comparing gremlin in your head say? How did it make you feel?

Dream Without Limits: Imagine you woke up tomorrow free of all self-doubt. (Wow, can we take a moment to say yaaasss to that feeling?!) What is the first creative thing you would do? Would you write a story, sing at the top of your lungs, sign up for that dance or pottery class, or start a DIY project you've been pinning on Pinterest? Describe it in juicy detail.

Your Unique Expression: Think of a time you expressed yourself and it felt so good. Maybe you journaled out your feelings, or you decorated your room exactly how you like it. What was special about that experience? What does it tell you about the ways you love to be creative?

Creative Role Models: Who's someone that inspires you with their creativity? (Could be a famous author, your quirky aunt, your friend who always has the best Instagram art, or even a fictional character.) What do you love about how they create or express themselves?

Fear vs. Freedom: What's one fear or belief about creativity that you're ready to let go of? (For example: "I'm not creative," "People will judge me," "It's a waste of time," etc.) How has this fear held you back? And how would your life feel different if you released it?

Take your time with these. Pour a cup of tea, play some calming music if you like, and let your pen flow like you're chatting with your best friend *(hey, that's me!)*. Remember, zero judgment—this journal is your safe space.

If any of these questions stir up emotions, it's okay. Breathe, maybe give yourself a little break, then come back when you're ready. You might uncover some beautiful truths about yourself and your creativity through this process. I'm right here cheering you on from the other side of these pages. ♡

Eliminate Creative Doubt: The 'Cut It Off' Method

Okay, now we're going to do something a little quirky and symbolic—but trust me, it's powerful. This is the "Cut It Off" release. It's a simple, physical way to say *"See ya!"* to the creative self-doubt or fear of judgment that's been lingering in your mind. Sometimes doing a real, tangible action helps our brains and hearts internalize the change. Plus, there's something oddly satisfying about literally cutting out negativity. *(Who knew arts-and-crafts time could be emotional healing time too?)*

Here's what we'll do, step by step, like two friends crafting together:

Step 1: Identify the Negative Nellies. Grab a blank sheet of paper and a pen. Take a moment to think about the biggest, meanest thoughts or beliefs that have been blocking your creative flow. You know, those nasty little voices like *"I'm not good at this," "People will laugh at me," "I'll never be as good as _____," or "Why bother? It won't be perfect."* Yeah, **those** guys. Write each of these self-doubting thoughts down on the paper. You can use big, ugly scribbles if you want, or write them in shaky handwriting—whatever matches how they make you feel. Get them all out onto that paper.

Step 2: Affirm the Opposite (Optional Bonus). This part is optional, but I find it empowering. Next to each ugly thought, write a bold truth or affirmation that counters it. For example, next to *"I'm not creative,"* you might write, *"I am creative in my own unique way, and it's valuable."* Next to *"People will judge me,"* maybe, *"The right people will celebrate my creativity, and my opinion of myself matters more."* This is like shining a light on each shadow—you're reminding yourself of what's true and positive. Even if you don't fully believe these affirmations yet, it's okay. We're planting seeds here.

Step 3: Cut, cut, cut! Now for the fun part. Take a pair of scissors *(safely, please!)* and cut up that paper. You can slice each sentence into its own strip, or chop the paper into confetti—whatever feels right. As you cut, imagine you are literally cutting those fears and doubts **out** of your life. They don't belong to you anymore. Say *goodbye!* You might even want to say out loud, *"I release you,"* or *"Not today, self-doubt!"*—or give a dramatic evil laugh—whatever makes you smile. The goal is to feel like you are reclaiming your power back from these thoughts.

Step 4: Trash it with *Gusto*. Now take those little slips or bits of paper and toss them in the trash or recycling bin. *Buh-bye!* Some friends of mine like to flush them down the toilet or even *(safely)* burn the paper in a fireplace as a ritual of release. Or maybe you want to stand up and throw them in the air like celebratory confetti for one last hurrah *(just remember to clean up after!)*. Do whatever feels symbolic to you. The key is that you're discarding those limiting beliefs. They are **not** welcome in your creative world anymore. Feel that weight lifting? That's you, getting lighter and freer!

After you've cut and discarded those doubts, close your eyes for a second. Take a deep breath in... and out. Notice how you feel. Maybe a bit relieved, maybe even a little giggly at the silliness of it, or perhaps empowered. You just told your fears who's boss in the most playful way. **You're the boss**, not those doubts. Remember that.

This "Cut It Off" ritual is something you can repeat anytime those pesky doubts start creeping back. It's like trimming off dead leaves so new growth can happen. And in this case, that new growth is your vibrant creativity, baby! Keep cutting off the junk that doesn't serve you, and keep nurturing what does. 🌱

Creative Exercise: Playful Expression Party

Now that we've kicked some self-doubt to the curb, let's have a little creative playtime, shall we? This is where we actively unleash that creativity we've been talking about. Don't worry, this is zero pressure, 100% fun. The goal here is to express yourself without any judgment—just pure, silly, joyful expression. Ready to have a mini creative party? *I am!*

Exercise: "Doodle Dance" (Music + Drawing + Movement)

This is one of my absolute favorite exercises because it combines music, art, and a bit of dance—three of my great loves. You can do this alone in your room, and you do **not** need to be "good" at drawing or dancing *(psst... what even is "good" when we're having fun?)*. Here's how:

1. **Set the Scene:** Grab a sheet of paper (or use the designed space two pages forward) and something to draw with—a pen, pencil, crayons, markers, lipstick, whatever you have. Next, pick a song that makes you feel happy or energized. Ideally something upbeat that you can't help but tap your foot to. It could be an old pop song that makes you nostalgic, a funky dance track, or even an instrumental piece that gives you all the feels. Press play and let the music fill your space.

2. **Doodle to the Beat:** As the music plays, start doodling on the paper in time with the music. There are no rules about what to draw—you're not aiming to create a "picture" of something. You're just letting your pen move with the rhythm. If it's a fast song, your pen might zigzag quickly. If it's slow and flowing, maybe you make long, swooping swirls. You might draw shapes, lines, dots, squiggles, even words or smiley faces—anything goes. The key is to let the music guide your pen, almost like your hand is dancing on the page.

3. **Add a Little Body Movement *(If You Want)*:** If you feel comfortable, try adding your own little dance into the mix. Maybe your shoulders sway or your head bops. You can even stand up and let your whole body move while you occasionally lean down to doodle on the paper that's on a table or the floor. This is truly about feeling

the music and letting your body and hand move together. It might feel silly—and that's great! Silly is welcome here with open arms. 🤗

4. **Don't Stop Till the Song Ends:** Keep doodling and dancing until your song ends. Immerse yourself in it. If one song ends and you're like *"Wait, I was in the zone!"* feel free to do another song. There's no rush and no rules. Go for as long as you're enjoying it.

5. **Reflect on Your Masterpiece:** When the music stops, take a look at your doodle-dance art. What do you see? It might look like wild nonsense, or maybe you'll notice it actually captures the mood of the song. The point is, you created something purely from your own playfulness. How do you feel now? A little more alive, a bit lighter? Did you laugh at any point or discover you love scribbling in neon pink highlighter? Whatever it is, note it down or just smile about it. This is what creative freedom feels like—fun, free, and uniquely you.

1. This exercise isn't about the outcome (the doodle) at all—it's about the process of letting go and creating joyfully. So high-five yourself *(literally give yourself a high-five, I won't judge!)* for participating. Each time you allow yourself to play like this, you're strengthening that creative muscle and proving to yourself that expression can be light-hearted and healing.

Feel free to try other playful expression activities too. You could sing in the shower like it's your private Broadway stage, or take goofy photos of your pets with funny captions, or try on outrageous outfits from your closet and strut around. Life is too short to be serious all the time. Embracing your creativity is like giving yourself permission to enjoy life's colors and flavors to the fullest. And oh boy, do you deserve that!

Keeping Creativity Alive: Clara's Self-Care Tips

Creativity, my dear, is like a little plant that thrives with some regular watering and sunshine. In other words, the more you nurture it, the more it grows and blossoms in your life.

Now that we've coaxed your creative spirit out to play, let's talk about how to keep it alive and happy as part of your everyday self-care routine. These are my personal tips—think of them as advice from your ever-enthusiastic best friend who really wants to see you shine:

- **Make Micro-Time for Creativity:** Life can get busy *(understatement of the year, right?)*. But you don't need hours of free time to be creative. Even 5-10 minutes a day of some fun, arty or crafty or expressive activity can light you up. Maybe you doodle in your planner, write a haiku while waiting for the coffee to brew, or hum a tune on your commute. Tiny pockets of creativity sprinkled through your day keep that spark glowing. It's like giving a little treat to your soul between all the adulting stuff.

1. **Create a Comforting Creative Space:** You don't need a fancy art studio—just a nook or even a little box of goodies will do. I have a "creativity corner" in my apartament, which is basically a comfy chair by the window and a basket filled with my journal, colorful pens, some washi tape, and stickers. Looking at those items makes me *want* to dive in. What could your creative setup be? Maybe a

shelf in your room with your sketchbook and watercolor set, or a playlist of karaoke songs ready to go. Set up your space or tools in a way that invites you: *"Come play with me!"*

2. **Remove the Pressure:** If you ever catch yourself thinking, *"What's the point of this?"* or *"I should be doing something productive instead,"* gently shush that thought. Your creativity is productive—it's feeding your soul, reducing stress, and making you happier. Not everything needs to result in a product or achievement. Remind yourself it's perfectly okay to do creative things just because they're fun or make you feel good. That reason is more than enough.

3. **Share if You Want *(or Don't)*:** Sometimes sharing our creative pursuits can amplify the joy. You might send a silly poem you wrote to your sister who needs a laugh, or cook that new recipe and invite a friend over to taste. Sharing can create beautiful moments of connection. But—and this is important—you are *not* obligated to share anything if you don't want to. If keeping a private journal or drawing just for you feels safer and more nourishing, that is completely valid. Do what makes your creative heart comfortable. This is self-care, not a performance.

- **Find Your Creative Tribe:** Surround yourself (physically or virtually) with people who encourage your creative side. Maybe it's a weekly crafting group, an online forum of writers, or just one friend who also loves scrapbooking or dancing in the kitchen. When you have folks who "get it," their energy can be contagious. You'll inspire each other, cheer each other on, and maybe even collaborate on fun projects. And if you're thinking, *"Eek, I don't know any creative people,"* I promise they're out there! Consider signing up for a local workshop or an online class in something you're curious about. You might meet your new artsy BFF there.

- **Celebrate Every Little Thing:** Made a silly sketch? **Celebrate it!** Wrote three lines in your journal? **Woohoo!** Hummed a melody that made you smile? Throw some metaphorical confetti! 🎉 What I'm saying is, acknowledge your creative moments and give yourself credit. It might feel goofy at first to pat yourself on the back for doodling a flower, but trust me, it trains your brain to recognize, *"Hey, creativity is a part of my life and it feels darn good."* The more you celebrate, the more you'll want to do it.

1. By weaving these practices into your life, you're treating your creativity as a beloved friend—one that's always been within you. Self-care isn't only bubble baths and meditation *(though those a—great too)*; it can also be laughing while painting polka dots on a canvas or tearing up magazines to make a vision board. The point is to keep that channel between your heart and your expression open and flowing. Consistency, kindness to yourself, and a sense of play—those are your secret ingredients.

Affirmations for Creativity & Self-Expression

Before we wrap up ou—reativity adventure, I want to leave you with some affirmations. Think of these as love notes to your creative soul. They're simple statements you can say to yourself to reinforce a positive mindset about your creativity and expression. You can whisper them in the morning, write them on sticky notes and stick them on your mirror, or repeat them in your mind whenever that mean self-doubt voice tries to butt in. I wrote these as if I'm speaking to you *(because I am!)*, but feel free to tweak the wording so it resonates perfectly with you:

- *I am a creative being, and my self-expression is a gift-not just to me, but to the world. There's no one else who creates quite like I do.*
- *I give myself permission to create without judgment or perfection. Messy, bold, quirky—it's all beautiful because it's from my heart.*
- *Every idea and spark I have is valuable. Even if it doesn't turn out as expected, it's still part of my journey and growth.*
- *I release the fear of what others might think. What I think and feel matters more. I create for me, and that is more than enough.*
- *Playing and creating bring me joy and healing. It's okay to have fun and be silly—in fact, it's wonderful! My creativity is a form of self-care.*
- *I am proud of my unique creativity. I cele—te my imagination and the way I see the world. It's safe for me to express myself.*
- *When I create, I connect with my true self. Each brush stroke, word, or dance move is me embracing who I am. And who I am is pretty amazing.*

- ***I trust my creative process.*** *It's okay if I don't know where it's going; I trust that something beautiful or meaningful will come out of it, even if that something is just learning about myself.*
- ***My creativity has no limits.*** *I am open to new inspiration every day, and I bravely follow my curiosity.*
- ***I am a creative powerhouse!*** *(Say this one with a big smile and power pose—hands on hips or fists in the air. Feel that energy? Yes, girl, that's you!)*

Pick one or two of these that really resonate and try starting your day with them for the next week. See how it feels. Or, if you have your journal nearby right now, circle or rewrite the ones that give you a little tingle of *"oooh, yes!"* in your belly or heart. Those tingles are your truth speaking up.

Whew! What a joyful ride this chapter has been. I'm so proud of you for sticking with me through this and for being open to exploring your creative side. You've listened to my stories, reflected on your own, bravely snipped away doubts, danced with doodles, and embraced new ways to care for that creative spark in you. That's a lot! Give yourself a big hug from me. 🤗

Always remember, your creativity isn't a frivolous extra—it's an essential part of you. It's your inner light, your best friend, your secret superpower. Whenever life feels gray or when you're a bit lost, I hope you turn to creativity as a way to find color and direction again. You don't have to be anyone else or meet any standard; just be **you** and express what's inside. That's more than enough.

Thank you for allowing me to share this personal chapter of my life and for trusting me as your guide and friend. I believe in you, and I believe in the magic you carry within. Now go on, beautiful, keep shining and creating. The world is so much brighter with your unique spark in it. ✨

Until next time, stay kind to yourself and keep that journal close—you never know when inspiration might strike!

With all my love and a splash of rainbow paint,

Clara

My creativity flows freely,
without limits or judgment.

6

Change and New Possibilities

Hello again, my brave friend! I can't believe we're already at Chapter 6. I'm so proud of how far you've come on this journey of letting go and growing. Today, I want to chat about embracing change and personal growth. It's a topic that used to scare me, but ending up *changing* my life *(pun intended!)*. And you know me by now—of course I have a personal story to share about it. Grab a cozy blanket or a cup of tea, and let's dive into how embracing change can open up wonderful new possibilities. Ready? Here we go.

Embracing Change in My Own Life

I'll never forget the summer when my life looked perfect from the outside, yet inside I felt completely stuck. Growing up, I had a life many people might dream of—a loving family, a beautiful home by the ocean, and all the comforts that come with a wealthy background. On the surface, it seemed like I had it all. But the truth? To be honest, I was **terrified of change** and secretly unhappy with the path I was on. I remember sitting on my balcony overlooking the Pacific, wondering why I felt so restless and empty when everything in my life was so "good" on paper. Crazy, right?

The turning point came in my mid-twenties. I was working at a job that I didn't love, staying in a relationship that felt safe but not fulfilling, and doing everything I thought I was "supposed" to do. I had spent years avoiding change because I was afraid to rock the boat. (*What if I made a mistake? What if I disappointed everyone?*) But one day, it hit me: **staying the same was actually scarier than taking a chance on something new.** I realized I was living a life that wasn't truly mine, and that realization both frightened and excited me.

One evening, after a long heart-to-heart talk with my best friend (over a big mug of tea, with tears and laughter), I decided I needed to take a leap. I quit that cushy job that was crushing my spirit. I gently ended the relationship that was holding us both back from real happiness. It was one of the hardest things I've ever done—I won't lie, I was shaking like a leaf and second-guessing myself the whole time—but it was also incredibly liberating. I felt like I had **cut off** the weights that were keeping me stuck in place.

In the months that followed, I experienced a lot of growing pains. Change isn't always smooth or easy, and there were moments I crawled under my covers thinking, *"Oh no, what have I done?!"* But day by day, I also felt myself blossoming. I started a small passion project helping other women, which eventually turned into the work I truly love *(yes, this journal is part of that!)*. I moved into a cozy little apartment that felt truly mine. I even took up surfing—something I'd always been curious about but never dared try—and found so much joy and peace in the waves. Each of these changes, both big and small, taught me that **embracing change was the key to finding myself.**

Looking back now, choosing to embrace change was the best decision I ever made for my personal growth. It wasn't glamorous or easy at first. There were tears, late-night ice cream sessions, and plenty of *"What the heck am I doing?"* moments. But through it all, I learned that I am braver and more resilient than I ever knew. Change became less of a monster under the bed and more of a friend knocking at the door, inviting me to step outside and see what's possible. And guess what? That's exactly what I want for you, too—to see that within every change lies a new possibility for you to grow into the amazing woman you are meant to be.

Grow Through Change: Why It's Essential

Let's chat about growth, you and I. Personal growth is one of those things that sounds really nice in theory *("becoming your best self" and all that jazz)*, but in reality it can feel uncomfortable, messy, and even scary. Change means stepping into the unknown, and we humans **love the familiar**—even if the familiar isn't making us happy. Trust me, I get it. There was a time I would have chosen my known, cozy rut over the scary unknown any day.

But here's the big secret I learned: **all the good stuff happens when you embrace change.** Think about it—every exciting opportunity, every lesson, every accomplishment in life usually started with something changing. Maybe it was a new job, a move to a different city, the end of a relationship, or even just a shift in your mindset. Change is the doorway that you walk through to discover who you can become. If we never walk through that door, we stay in one room forever. *(And hey, even if that room is nicely decorated, it gets stuffy after a while, right?)*

Embracing change is really about believing in yourself and your capacity to adapt. It's okay to feel nervous—that means you're on the edge of something that matters to you. When you face a change, big or small, and say *"Okay, I'm going to try,"* you're telling yourself that growth is possible. You don't have to have it all figured out *(nobody gets a perfect map for life)*. In fact, learning as you go is part of the fun *(even if it doesn't feel fun 100% of the time)*. Each little step into new territory teaches you that you can handle more than you thought.

And guess what? Every time you embrace change, you build confidence for the next time. It's like working out a muscle—the *"I can handle this"* muscle. The first time you really use it, you might be sore (oh boy, *was I sore* after leaving my old life behind!). But then you try another change—maybe a small one, like taking a new class or setting a boundary—and that muscle gets stronger. Over time, change starts to feel a bit less intimidating. You realize that you've been capable of handling more than you ever gave yourself credit for.

I promise, it's worth it—and you're not doing it alone. **I'm right here cheering you on**, like the devoted friend I am.

Reflection & Journaling Prompts: Your Growth Journey

Now, let's turn the spotlight to *you*, my dear. This is where you get to explore your own growth journey. There's no rush and no pressure—just you being honest with yourself, like we're two friends having a heart-to-heart. Grab your pen and consider these gentle questions. Remember, there are no right or wrong answers. Write whatever comes to mind, and be kind to yourself in the process.

• • •

What is a change in your life that you've been afraid to embrace? Maybe it's something big like a new career path, or something more personal like setting a boundary or exploring a new hobby. What about it feels scary or uncertain?

Can you think of a time when you did embrace change or try something new? How did it turn out, and how did you feel afterward? Sometimes looking back at even small changes (like joining a club, making a new friend, or speaking up for yourself) can remind you that you are capable of growth.

What do you imagine is on the other side of the change you fear? *Close your eyes and picture the best possible outcome. If you took that leap, what new possibilities might open up for you? How might you feel about yourself?*

Are there any "comfort zones" in your life that have started to feel limiting? *Describe what they are. How might it feel to gently expand those walls and try something a little outside of them?*

What support do you need to embrace the changes you want?
Think about people, resources, or self-reminders that could help. It's okay to ask for help or seek encouragement—growth doesn't have to be a solo journey.

Take your time with these prompts. Pour yourself another cup of coffee or tea, find a cozy spot, and just let your thoughts flow. I'm right there with you in spirit, nodding and smiling as you write. This is your space to dream about the growth you crave and to acknowledge the fears that have been holding you back. Sometimes just putting it all on paper can bring a sense of relief and clarity.

The "Cut It Off" Release: Fire-Based Ritual—Burn Away Your Fear

Writing down your fears and burning the paper is a cathartic way to release them. Fire is a powerful symbol of purification and transformation. In this exercise, **you'll "cut off" and release your fear by burning it**—quite literally turning your fear into ash. It's a bold, dramatic ritual that feels deeply personal: as you watch the flames consume what you wrote, you symbolically destroy the fear's hold over you. This method can be incredibly cathartic, leaving you with a renewed sense of freedom and resolve.

Steps:

1. **Gather what you need:** You'll need a pen, paper, and a safe way to burn the paper. This could be a fireplace, a metal/glass bowl or pot, or an outdoor space where a small fire is allowed. Have some water or a fire extinguisher nearby for safety, and tie back any long hair or loose clothing. Create a calm environment—dim the lights if indoors, or do this at dusk if outside, to make the ritual feel sacred.

2. **Write down your fear:** Sit with the paper and pen and **start pouring out your fear onto the page.** Be as specific and honest as you can. You might write a letter addressed to your fear, or simply list the things that scare you and you're ready to release. For example, *"I am afraid of ___, but it no longer protects or serves me. I release this fear."* The act of writing externalizes the fear, getting it out of your head and into a form you can destroy. Take your time until you feel you've captured the essence of what you want to let go.

3. **Set a clear intention to let it go:** Read over what you wrote. Acknowledge those feelings—it's okay to feel a twinge of that fear as you see it on paper. Now take a moment and declare (out loud or in your mind): *"I am ready to release this fear."* By affirming this, you're cementing your desire to be free of it. Fold the paper up when you're ready, as a little package of fear that you're about to toss away for good.

4. **Burn the fear paper:** Place the paper in your fire-safe container or designated spot. Light a match or use a lighter to carefully set the paper on fire *(always minding safety)*. As the paper catches fire, **watch the flames** grow and consume the words you wrote. **Imagine the fear itself being burned away.** You might say a final phrase as it burns, such as *"Begone, fear"* or *"I release you,"* or simply focus on the visual of the fire doing the work. Allow any emotions to rise—you might feel a sense of power, or even a rush of relief or tears.

5. **Dispose of the ashes:** Once the paper has completely turned to ash and the fire is out, take a moment to observe the ashes—the fear is now nothing but powdery remnants. When it's cool, scatter the ashes to the wind outdoors, or wash them down the sink/drain with

water. This final act **ensures the fear is truly gone** from your life. As you dispose of the ashes, feel the finality of it: you have *cut off* that fear and it can no longer affect you.

6. **Reflect and reinforce:** Take a deep breath and notice how you feel with that fear burned away. Most people feel a mix of liberation, relief, and empowerment at this point. To reinforce your new fearless state, you can write down a positive statement or an opposite of that fear in the space below (for example, "I am courageous and open to new experiences"). Keep this as an empowering reminder of the change you just made.

• • •

Why it works: There is real psychology behind *"write it down and destroy it"* exercises. By writing down a fear, you take it out of your mind and make it tangible. When you physically destroy that paper, your brain gets the message that the fear is also being destroyed. In fact, research shows that when people write down negative thoughts and then throw them away, they tend to mentally discard those thoughts afterward. Burning is a particularly strong form of discarding—it's fast, visual, and irreversible. As you watch the paper turn to ash, you experience a powerful sense of finality. *Symbolically,* fire represents purification and transformation; many healing traditions use burning ceremonies to cleanse negativity. As one guide explains, *"As it turns to ash, let it go and make room for new possibilities."*. This ritual is empowering because **you take control** of the fear by literally destroying it. It turns fear from something internal and intimidating into something external that you can crumble and burn. When it's over, the fear that once weighed on your heart is now just ashes on the wind—a clear sign that you've **cut off its power over you.**

Creative Exercise: Your Growth Vision Board

Now that you've started letting go of fear, let's fill that space with some inspiration and vision! One of my favorite ways to get excited about personal growth is to create a **Growth Vision Board.** This is a fun, artsy way to visualize the changes and new possibilities you want in your life. Think of it like making a collage of your future—one where you're blooming, learning, and stepping into your best self. *(And don't worry, you don't have to be super artistic for this—it's about meaning, not perfection.)*

How to create your Growth Vision Board:

1. **Gather your materials.** You'll need a piece of poster board or paper *(even a page in your notebook will do)*, some old magazines, newspapers or printed images, scissors, glue or tape, and maybe some markers or pens. If you're more into digital creations, you can even make a digital collage on your phone or computer using Pinterest or a collage app.

2. **Set the mood.** Find a comfy spot and put on your favorite music. Make this a fun, relaxing activity. You could even invite a friend to join you if you want company *(vision board party, anyone?)*.

3. **Reflect on your growth goals.** Before you start cutting and gluing, take a moment to think about the personal growth you want to embrace. How do you want to change? What new experiences do you want? How do you want to feel as you grow? Maybe you want to be more confident, or learn a new skill, or move to a new place—anything that lights you up. Picture it in your mind.

4. **Find images and words that inspire you.** Flip through those magazines or search online for pictures that represent the changes and growth you desire. Look for images that give you that little thrill of excitement or hope. It could be a picture of someone climbing a mountain *(symbolizing overcoming challenges)*, a serene beach *(peace and new horizons)*, a butterfly *(transformation)*, a graduation cap *(learning)*, or even words like "courage" or "thriving." Choose whatever resonates with you personally.

5. **Create your collage.** Cut out the images and words you found and start arranging them on your board or paper. There's no "right" way to do this—you can make it neat and orderly, or wild and patchwork. Glue or tape everything down once you're happy with the layout. You can also add your own words or little doodles if you're feeling creative. This board is all about you, so let your personality shine.

6. **Put it on display.** When you're done, take a moment to really look at your vision board. Isn't it beautiful? This collage is a visual representation of where you're headed and all the wonderful growth ahead of you. Place your board somewhere you can see it often—maybe on your bedroom wall, by your mirror, or as the

background on your phone. Every time you see it, it'll remind you of the path you're on and keep you motivated.

I absolutely love making vision boards because they make my dreams feel tangible and real. When I was stepping into my new life after leaving my old one behind, I made a vision board filled with images of strong, happy women, inspiring quotes, and little things I wanted to welcome into my life *(yes, I included a picture of a surfer girl riding a wave!)*. I can't tell you how uplifting it was to see those images every day. It kept me focused on where I wanted to go, especially on days when I felt a bit lost or doubtful. So have fun with this, and let yourself dream big. You **deserve** to envision a future that excites you.

Self-Care Strategies: Supporting Your Growth

As your virtual best friend, I want to make sure you have all the support you need as you embrace change and grow. Self-care is so important during times of growth because, let's face it, change can be exhausting and emotional. Taking care of yourself isn't just bubble baths and candles *(though those are wonderful too)*; it's also about nurturing your mind and soul so you can keep going forward. Here are some of my favorite self-care strategies to maintain and reinforce your personal growth:

- **Be patient and gentle with yourself.** Growth doesn't happen overnight, and it's definitely not a straight line. You'll have good days where you feel like an unstoppable rockstar, and other days where you want to hide under the covers. Both are okay! Remind yourself that ups and downs are normal. Talk to yourself the way I would talk to you: with kindness, encouragement, and zero judgment.

- **Celebrate small wins.** Did you step a teeny bit out of your comfort zone today? *High five!* Maybe you spoke up in a meeting, or signed up for that online class, or even just thought about making a change. No achievement is too small to celebrate. Treat yourself to something nice or do a little happy dance. Acknowledging progress *(no matter how tiny)* builds confidence and makes the journey fun.

- **Keep a "growth" journal.** Since this is a guided journal, you're already journaling *(go you!)*. Continue to use journaling as a safe space to vent your fears and also to record your victories and insights. When you're feeling uncertain, flip back through your journal and see how far you've come. It's so powerful to have a written record of your own evolution—it's like evidence that yes, you **are** growing and learning, even if it's hard to see in the moment.

- **Stay connected with supportive people.** You don't have to do this alone. Share your goals or the changes you're working on with a trusted friend, family member, or even a support group *(online communities count too!)*. Let them cheer you on and give you pep talks. Sometimes when our own belief wavers, hearing *"You've got this"* from someone who cares can make all the difference. And if you encounter naysayers or people who aren't supportive... remember that says more about their fears than about you. Stick with your cheerleaders.

- **Practice stress relief.** Change—even positive change—can stir up stress and anxiety. Make sure you have go-to activities that calm you and refill your cup. This could be taking walks, doing yoga or stretching, meditating for a few minutes, praying if that's meaningful to you, or just blasting your favorite music and singing in the shower. *(I personally have a playlist of songs that make me feel like I can conquer the world—highly recommend making one!)*. Taking care of your emotional well-being will give you the strength to keep moving forward.

- **Remind yourself of your *"why."*** On tough days, reconnect with the reason you're embracing change in the first place. Maybe you're doing it to be happier, to set a good example for your kids, to live without regrets, or simply because you owe it to yourself to live fully. Write your "why" on a sticky note or in a note on your phone. When fear or doubt creeps in, revisit that reason. It's your personal motivation fuel.

- **Set boundaries when needed.** As you grow, you might notice certain people or environments that drain you or make you doubt yourself. It's okay to take a step back from anything (or anyone) that isn't supporting your journey. Think of it as pruning a garden—sometimes you have to cut off the weeds to let the flowers thrive. Give yourself permission to protect your peace. It's an act of self-love, not selfishness.

Remember, self-care is not a one-time thing; it's a continuous practice, especially when you're pushing your limits and trying new things. Whenever you feel overwhelmed, come back to these basics: rest, reflect, reach out, and remind yourself that you are doing the best you can. I'm so proud of you for every bit of effort you're putting into your growth. You deserve all the love and care—*especially* from yourself.

Affirmations for Personal Growth

I'm a big believer in the power of affirmations—those little positive statements that can help rewire our thinking. Think of them as love notes to your future self. They might feel a tad cheesy at first *(I used to roll my eyes at affirmations, to be honest)*, but give them a chance. Repeating affirmations can gradually replace some of those fearful or negative thoughts with empowering ones. Here are some of my favorite affirmations for embracing change and personal growth. Feel free to borrow them or tweak them to fit what feels true for you:

- *I welcome change as a chance to grow and discover more about myself.*
- *I am capable of adapting and learning through every new experience.*
- *With every step I take into the unknown, I become stronger and wiser.*
- *I release the fear of what could go wrong and focus on the exciting possibilities ahead.*
- *I trust myself to handle whatever comes my way, because I've gotten through challenges before.*
- *Every day, in small ways, I am growing and becoming the woman I want to be.*
- *Change brings me closer to my authentic self.*
- *I embrace new beginnings and trust the journey of my life.*
- *I deserve to pursue what makes me truly happy and fulfilled.*
- *I am proud of myself for being brave and trying new things.*

You can write these down on sticky notes, jot them in your journal, or even say them to yourself in the mirror each morning *(yes, it feels weird at first, but it can also be oddly powerful—I've definitely given myself a pep talk in the bathroom mirror more than once!)*. The key is to repeat the ones that resonate with you regularly. Over time, you'll find that these positive thoughts come more naturally, especially when you're faced with a new challenge. Instead of immediately thinking *"I can't,"* you'll start hearing a little voice in your head say, *"Maybe I can, actually!"*

Embracing New Possibilities: You've Got This!

Take a moment to soak all of this in, my dear. Personal growth is a journey—one that lasts a lifetime. And here you are, bravely stepping forward, one foot *(or maybe one toe)* out of your comfort zone at a time. I hope this chapter has shown you that change, while a bit intimidating, is also incredibly rewarding. It's the path that leads you to new possibilities, to discovering strengths you didn't know you had, and to living a life that feels true to you.

Remember, I'm right here with you in spirit, cheering on every little victory—and consoling you on the hard days. We're in this together, and I believe in you with all my heart. Whenever you feel unsure, come back to these pages. Re-read the story, do the exercises again, or just remind yourself of the affirmations and the vision you have. Growth isn't a straight line, but with each twist and turn, you are learning and becoming.

You are stronger, braver, and more amazing than you know. Change might be knocking—go ahead and open the door, even if your hand shakes a little. The *you* that emerges on the other side will be so grateful that you did.

Now, let's take a deep breath together. Inhale that fresh, hopeful air of new beginnings... and exhale any lingering doubt. ***You've got this.*** Onward to all the wonderful new adventures and possibilities that await you!

With all my love and a hopeful heart,

*I am becoming the bravest,
most authentic
version of myself.*

7

Gratitude and Positivity

Finding Light in My Rich Sad Life

I have a confession, my friend: I didn't always understand gratitude. On the outside, my life looked pretty perfect. I grew up with a loving family and plenty of comfort, so by all accounts I *should* have been happy. But inside, I often felt a quiet emptiness I couldn't explain. I remember sitting on the beach one golden evening, watching the waves roll in, and feeling nothing but stress about everything that wasn't right in my life.

For a long time, I focused on what I lacked. If a friend forgot to call me back, I'd dwell on feeling ignored. If I got a scratch on my car, I'd obsess over it for days. I had so much to be grateful for, yet I zeroed in on the little negatives. *Can you relate?* Maybe you've had moments like that too—where ten things go well but one thing goes wrong and that one thing steals the show in your mind. That was me, all the time. I was caught in a cycle of seeing the glass half-empty, even though my life overflowed in so many ways.

My wake-up call came during a particularly rough patch. I had just gone through a painful breakup—the kind that makes you want to stay in bed all day with the covers over your head. Instead of appreciating the friends who showed up for me or the comfort of being with family *(which I had definitely taken for granted)*, all I could think about was what I'd lost. I felt so low that even the Newport Beach sunsets I used to love looked gray to me. One night, as I sat on the porch feeling completely sorry for myself, my older sister joined me. She handed me a small journal *(This was my first contact with such thing—honestly, I rolled my eyes at first)*. She said, *"Clara, each night I want you to write down three things—just three—that you're grateful for, even if today was hard."* I grumbled something like, *"We'll see,"* but inside I was curious. I mean, I was desperate to feel better. So I tried it.

At first, I struggled. My pen hovered over the page while my mind went blank. *What on earth am I grateful for right now?* I wondered. Eventually, I scribbled a few simple things: *"I'm grateful for my sister's hug. I'm grateful I watched a funny show that made me laugh through my tears.*

I'm grateful for the sound of ocean waves tonight." They were small things, but you know what? I felt a tiny flicker of warmth in my chest after writing them. It wasn't an overnight transformation—I didn't suddenly become *Little Miss Sunshine* the next morning. But day by day, that practice of focusing on little blessings started shifting something in me. I noticed the beautiful pink sunrise on my drive to work and silently said thanks instead of ignoring it. I appreciated that my body got me out of bed even when my heart felt heavy. Slowly, the gray fog began to lift, and I could feel color in my life again. That's when I learned the real power of gratitude: it's like adjusting a camera lens to bring the good things into focus. The good was always there—I just had to choose to see it. And wow, my friend, once you *learn* to see it, life becomes so much more vibrant.

Understanding Gratitude & Positivity: Why Shifting Focus Changes Everything

Let's talk about what I discovered in that little gratitude journal experiment. Gratitude isn't about ignoring the bad or plastering on a fake smile—trust me, I'm all about being real with our feelings. Instead, gratitude is about gently training our minds to also see the good that lives alongside the challenges. It's like being a treasure hunter in your own life, looking for gems even on the rough days.

When you practice gratitude, you're essentially saying, "Okay, I acknowledge things are tough *and* I can still find a sliver of light." That shift in focus is life-changing. It was for me, and I believe it can be for you too.

Why is gratitude such a big deal? For one, it flips the script in our heads. Our brains naturally tend to cling to negative events *(it's a survival thing from way back when we needed to remember which berries not to eat)*. But in modern life, that can leave us obsessing over a rude comment or a mistake at work, while forgetting the twenty other nice things that happened. Practicing gratitude is like giving your brain a loving nudge: *"Hey, look over here at this good thing!"* Over time, those nudges train your mind to spotlight the positives more easily. And believe me, that doesn't just make you happier—it can actually ease stress and anxiety. I noticed that on days I listed what I appreciated, I went to bed calmer. Instead of my mind racing with worries, it was mellowed by thoughts of, say, how comfy my pillows felt or how grateful I was for my dog's unconditional love.

Incorporating positivity into daily life can be simple *(and even fun!)*. It's not about huge gestures; it's the little moments. For example, I started a habit of mentally saying "thank you" every time I took my first sip of coffee in the morning. I know it might sound silly, but that warm mug in my hands became my tiny daily ritual of positivity. I'd think, *"Thank you for this delicious coffee. Thank you for a new day."* Starting the morning that way set a softer tone for everything that followed. Gratitude can be woven into anything: your commute *("thank you for this podcast making traffic bearable")*, your meals *("thank you for this yummy sandwich")*, or even your interactions *("thank you to that stranger who held the door open")*. Bit by bit, you find yourself noticing more of what's going *right* than what's going wrong. And that, my dear friend, feels empowering. It's like switching on a light in a dark room—suddenly you can see the lovely things that were hidden in the shadows.

Positivity naturally blossoms from a grateful heart. When you practice appreciation, you're essentially watering the seeds of positivity in your mind. It doesn't mean you'll never have negative thoughts *(we're human, not robots!)*. But it means those negative thoughts won't control the show as often. You'll have a tool to balance them. For example, now when I catch myself spiraling—say I start thinking, *"Ugh, I'm so behind on everything, I'm a mess"*—I pause and deliberately find one good thing: *"Actually, I got through a tough day and I'm still here trying. That's something to be proud of."* That positive reframe, rooted in self-appreciation, can cut through the gloom. Gratitude gives you perspective. It reminds you that life isn't all bad or all good; it's a mix, and we have the power to choose what to magnify. How amazing is that? We might not control every event in life, but we *can* influence what we focus on. And where focus goes, energy flows. When you focus on gratitude and positivity, you invite more of that good energy into your life. I've seen it in my own journey, and I'm so excited for you to experience it too, one small thankful moment at a time.

Reflection & Journaling Prompts: Your Gratitude Journey

Alright, now it's your turn, lovely. Let's gently explore your world through a lens of gratitude. Grab your colorful pens, or just sit with these questions in your mind. There's no "right" answer, no pressure—just a heart-to-heart between you and you. Imagine me there with you, maybe with a cup of tea in hand, asking these questions softly like a curious friend. Take your time with them, and be honest with yourself. You might be surprised by what you discover:

• • •

Think of a small, simple thing that brought you a bit of joy today (even if today was hard). What was it, and how did it make you feel in that moment?

Who is someone you're grateful to have in your life right now?
What do you appreciate about them? How might you let them know they matter to you?

Recall a challenge or tough experience you've been through. Can you find a silver lining or a lesson from it that you're thankful for now? *(It's okay if you're not there yet—take your time.)*

What are three things you often take for granted in your daily life that, if you really think about it, you deeply appreciate?
(Think super simple: the roof over your head, your favorite comfy socks, your ability to read these words.)

How do you feel when you focus on what you're grateful for, even if it's just for a minute? *Describe that feeling—warm, calm, hopeful?—and note where you feel it in your body.*

As you reflect or jot down your answers, remember: there are no wrong answers. This is for *you*. If some of these gratitude prompts are hard to answer because you're going through a lot right now, that's okay. Be gentle with yourself. Even acknowledging *"This is hard right now, but I'm glad I'm trying"* is a form of gratitude—gratitude for your own courage. Every little step counts.

The "Cut It Off" Release: Cutting the Ties of Negativity

Now let's do a little release ritual—by now, you know I love these meaningful, symbolic gestures! Since this chapter is all about shifting focus to appreciation, we'll start by literally cutting off some negativity to make space for more gratitude in your heart. Don't worry, this is pretty simple *(and even a bit fun)*. Here's what I suggest:

1. **Gather a *"tie"* to cut.** Grab a piece of string or yarn (a piece a few inches long works). If you don't have string handy, you can even cut a long strip of paper to stand in as your "string." Find a quiet moment and think of a negative thought pattern or worry that's been nagging at you—the kind of negativity you'd like to let go of. Maybe it's a self-criticism like *"I'm not good enough,"* or a gloomy thought like *"Nothing ever goes right for me."* We all have one *(or a few)* of those. If you have more than one in mind, that's okay; you can tackle a couple. Now, tie a knot in your string for each negative thought or feeling you're ready to release. As you tie each knot, you might even whisper or think about what that knot represents (for example, *"this knot is my fear of failure"*).

2. **Cut through the negativity.** Take a deep breath and hold that knotted string. These knots symbolize the negative thoughts tying you up. Now for the satisfying part: grab your scissors. One by one, cut right through each knot on your string. *(If it's easier, you can snip the string just above and below the knot to completely remove that little knotted piece.)* As you make each cut, imagine you are severing that negative thought's hold on you. You can even say out loud *(or in your head)*, *"I am cutting off this negativity. It does not serve me."* You are the boss of your own mind, and you have the right to evict any thought that brings you down. Feel free to be as dramatic as you want here—sometimes I literally say *"goodbye!"* as I snip through a knot. Do whatever helps you feel empowered as you cut those ties.

3. **Let it go—for real.** Gather up the little pieces you cut off (those knotted bits of string). Now, get rid of them in a way that feels good to you. You might toss them decisively into the trash can, or even flush them away if they're just paper. If you're the ceremonious type and it's safe to do so, you could burn the pieces *carefully* in a fireplace or sink *(watch those fingers and only do this in a controlled, safe way!)*. As you dispose of each piece, picture the negative thought it represented *leaving* your life. Say ***"good riddance"*** if it makes you smile. The point is to physically and mentally release those negative bits and declare that they're not welcome to clutter your mind anymore.

4. **Invite a positive fill-in.** Now that you've cut off those negative ties, let's fill that open space with a dose of positivity. Take another deep breath. Think of something good to focus on—maybe a positive thought or an uplifting truth you want to remember. It could be as simple as, *"I am capable and I am learning,"* or *"I'm grateful for [something or someone] in my life."* You can say it out loud or just in your heart. If you feel like it, you can even write this positive statement down bellow or on a new slip of paper and keep it somewhere visible (tape it to your mirror or tuck it in your wallet). Do whatever helps the idea sink in. Now, take a moment to notice how you feel after doing all this. A bit lighter? A bit more hopeful or free? I hope so. I'm **so proud of you** for trying this exercise and honoring yourself in this way.

This "Cut It Off" release might seem simple, but it's sending a powerful message to yourself: *you are choosing to let go of thoughts that weigh you down.* Whenever negative thoughts start creeping back, remember this little ritual (you can even do it again anytime you need). Each time you physically cut off something that doesn't serve you, you reinforce the truth that ***you hold the scissors***—you have the power to cut off what isn't helping you. And in that freed-up space, you can welcome in more gratitude and positivity. *How empowering is that?*

Creative Exercise: Gratitude in Action

Gratitude isn't just a feeling, it's something we *do*—an action, a way of life. One of the most enjoyable ways I found to weave gratitude into my daily routine was by turning it into a little creative project. As your self-appointed best friend, I've got a lovely idea for you to try. Feel free to tweak it or make it your own. The goal is simply to actively practice appreciation in a way that feels engaging. Ready? Here's a suggestion:

Start a "Gratitude Jar" ***(with a twist).*** Find any jar or box *(it doesn't have to be fancy—an empty jam jar, a shoebox, whatever you have is perfect)*. Each day for the next week *(or month, or hey, the next year!)*, write down one thing you're grateful for on a small slip of paper and drop it in the jar. But here's the twist: also include *why* you're grateful for it. For example, instead of just "I'm grateful for my friend Sarah," write *"I'm grateful for my friend Sarah* ***because*** *she always makes me laugh when I need it."* Or *"I'm grateful for my morning jog* ***because*** *it clears my mind and makes me feel strong."* Adding the "why" makes the gratitude feel even more real and deep. It's like you're not only noticing the gift, you're acknowledging the impact it has on you.

Make this a fun daily ritual. Maybe every evening before bed, you take a quiet minute to reflect on the day and pick your gratitude highlight. Or each morning with your coffee, you think of one thing from yesterday that you appreciate. If you miss a day, no guilt—this isn't a homework assignment, it's a loving habit you're cultivating. On days when you're feeling blue, challenge yourself to find *something* **(even something tiny)** to add to the jar. Some days might be as simple as *"I'm grateful for a warm blanket on a cold night"*—that totally counts!

Here's the best part: whenever you're in need of a pick-me-up, go to your jar and pull out a few slips to read. It's like reaching into a cookie jar, but instead of cookies, you're getting sweet reminders of good things in your life. *(Gratitude cookies, zero calories, all the warmth!* 😉*)* Reading through those little notes—*especially* the reasons why you're grateful—can instantly shift your mood. I keep my Gratitude Jar on my bookshelf, and on those days I feel *"meh"* or start dwelling on the negative, I grab a handful of my past gratitude notes. I can't even tell you how much it helps to physically see dozens of happy moments and blessings I've acknowledged. It's like a tangible pile of positivity that **you** created for yourself. Magic.

If a jar isn't your style, there are plenty of other ways to put gratitude into action creatively. You could keep a gratitude board—pin up photos or Post-its of things you love. Or make a playlist of songs that make you feel thankful to be alive. Or set a daily alarm on your phone that reminds you: *"Pause, breathe, and find one thing you appreciate right now."* There are so many possibilities. The key is to make gratitude a practice, something you do regularly in a way that brings you joy. Because the more you practice, the easier it gets, and the more it just becomes part of who you are. And I can't think of a more beautiful trait to have than a grateful heart.

Gratitude Practices: Boosting Your Emotional Well-Being

Gratitude is like a superpower in your self-care toolkit. It's not just about saying "thanks"—it's a form of self-love and emotional nourishment. When life gets stressful or your confidence feels wobbly, leaning into gratitude can be a comforting and empowering form of self-care. Let me share some of my best-friend tips on using gratitude and positive thinking to take care of your gorgeous soul:

- **Start and end your day with a grateful thought:** Before you reach for your phone in the morning, take a moment to think of one thing you're grateful for. It could be as simple as, "I'm grateful I get a fresh start today." And each night, despite how the day went, find one thing to say thank you for *(even if it's "I made it through today"—that counts!)*. This gentle bookend of gratitude can cushion your day in positivity.
- **Use gratitude as a mood reset button:** When you're feeling anxious, sad, or irritated, pause and take a deep breath. Ask yourself,

"What is one good thing in this moment?" It might be hard to see at first, especially if your emotions are strong. Maybe the only thing you can think of is "I'm grateful for this breath," or "I'm grateful for the quiet of this room"—and that is okay. By doing this, you're not dismissing your feelings; you're soothing them. It's like telling your nervous system, *"Hey, there is safety and goodness here, too."* This little practice has saved me from many a meltdown, I promise.

- **Express gratitude to others as self-care:** This might sound backwards—shouldn't self-care be about *me*, not others? But here's the magic: when you express appreciation to someone else, it creates a beautiful boomerang of positivity. Send a quick text to a friend saying you're thankful for their presence in your life, or thank your coworker for their help, or tell your mom how much you value her. Notice how you feel afterward. Personally, I always feel a rush of warmth and connection when I do this. It reminds me I'm not alone and that I have support and love around me—which is so important for our well-being. Connection is self-care, and gratitude strengthens our connections.

- **Practice self-gratitude:** This one's a game-changer, so listen up. Self-gratitude means appreciating *yourself*. We're so good at beating ourselves up, but how often do we thank *ourselves*? Try this: look in the mirror and thank yourself for something. It could be, "Thank you, [your name], for showing up today even though it was hard," or "I'm grateful to myself for my creativity," or even, *"I appreciate my body for carrying me through the day."* At first it might feel awkward, but it's incredibly nourishing. You deserve your own kindness. Being grateful for who you are is the ultimate self-care, because you are with you 24/7. That relationship deserves gratitude and love.

- **Surround yourself with positive reminders:** This is a practical little tip. Keep gratitude visible in your environment. Maybe it's sticky notes with uplifting quotes on your bathroom mirror, or a beautiful wallpaper on your phone that reminds you of something you love. I have a small rock on my desk that says "gratitude" *(I found it in a gift shop—it's just a pebble with the word engraved on it)*. When I see it while I'm working, it gently brings me back to an appreciative mindset, especially on tough days. Little visual cues can nudge you toward positivity without you even realizing it. It's like setting up your space to be your cheerleader.

•

Remember, using gratitude as self-care doesn't mean you ignore problems or paste a smiley face over pain. It means you give yourself the gift of noticing hope and goodness, especially when you're struggling. It's one of the most loving things you can do for yourself. You're training your mind to be kinder and more supportive—and you totally deserve that kindness.

Affirmations for Gratitude & Positivity

To wrap up this chapter, I want to share some affirmations—think of them as little love notes to remind your mind to focus on abundance and positivity. You can say these to yourself in the morning, write them on your mirror, repeat them in your head during the day, or whisper them at night before sleep. I often speak mine while I'm driving *(hands on the wheel, heart on my sleeve, ha!)*. Choose one or two that resonate with you, or craft your own. Say them with feeling, and trust that over time, their message will sink in. Here are a few of my favorites:

- *I am grateful for the abundance of goodness in my life, both big and small.*
- *My life is filled with blessings, and I choose to notice and appreciate them.*
- *I release negative thoughts and welcome positive, uplifting energy into my mind.*
- *Each day I find new reasons to smile and say thank you.*
- *I focus on what I can appreciate in this moment, and it brings me peace.*
- *My heart is open to joy, gratitude, and beautiful possibilities.*

Repeat these affirmations whenever you need a dose of positivity. Feel the truth in the words: you are cultivating a more grateful, positive mindset, bit by bit. Every time you affirm goodness, you're training your brain to lean into the light.

Closing Thoughts: Embracing Gratitude Every Day

Shifting your focus to appreciation and positive thinking is a journey, and I'm so honored to be on this journey with you. Remember, my dear friend, gratitude is always there for you like a comforting hug on a hard day. When you intentionally look for things to be grateful for, you're not denying life's difficulties—you're reminding yourself that hope and joy still exist *amidst* the challenges. You have the power to choose what you magnify in your life. And from what I've seen, when you magnify the good, the good grows.

I'm cheering you on as you cultivate this gratitude practice. I've seen it work wonders in my own life—turning my outlook from gray to a whole spectrum of colors—and I have absolute faith it will bring beautiful changes to yours, too. Be patient and gentle with yourself. Some days will be easier than others, and that's okay. Keep cutting off the negative when it creeps in, keep inviting the positive, and know that every single attempt you make to shift your focus is an act of self-love.

You deserve all the light and happiness a grateful heart can bring. Here's to appreciating today, glowing with positivity, and stepping into tomorrow with hope. I'm grateful for you—yes, *you*—for reading this and allowing me to share this piece of my heart. Now, let's go forth and count our blessings, one genuine "thank you" at a time.

8

Empowerment

Hello, my dear one. I'm so excited to dive into this chapter because it's all about recognizing your own strength and stepping into your personal power. To kick things off, I want to share a personal story that's very close to my heart.

On the outside, a few years ago I seemed to have everything under control. I had landed a great job at a well-known company right out of college—the kind of job that made my family and friends proud. I wore the professional wardrobe, attended the big meetings, and by all accounts, I was "successful." But inside, I often felt surprisingly small and unfulfilled. While everyone thought I was thriving, I knew something was missing. I would sit in meetings afraid to voice my ideas, and I'd go home every night feeling drained. All that external success didn't magically give me confidence or a sense of purpose. In truth, I was living a life that looked perfect on paper but didn't feel true to me.

One of the hardest and bravest moments of my life came when I decided to walk away from that "perfect" path. I remember one afternoon in particular: I had pitched a creative idea in a team meeting—an idea I was really excited about. My boss gave me a polite smile and then promptly moved on to the next topic as if I hadn't spoken at all. It seems like a small thing, but in that moment I felt completely invisible and undervalued. It was the last straw after years of feeling like I had to **tone myself down** to fit other people's expectations.

That evening, I sat alone at my desk long after office hours, my heart pounding in the quiet. A voice inside me that I'd been shushing for years finally said, *Enough*. I realized I had dreams of my own—projects I wanted to create, work that would make me leap out of bed with excitement—but I'd been too afraid to go after them. I was so worried about disappointing others and clinging to my sense of stability that I had **silenced my own aspirations.** With trembling hands, I began typing out a resignation letter. I didn't send it right away, but just writing it made that inner voice roar even louder. Within a week, after many late-night soul-searching sessions, I made one of the boldest decisions of my life: ***I quit my job.***

Let me tell you, handing in that resignation was absolutely terrifying. I was literally shaking as I informed my boss, and I had to fight back tears of anxiety even though deep down I knew it was right. My family was shocked—some of them thought I'd lost my mind by walking away from a good salary and a "safe" career. Friends asked if I was really sure and whether I had some big plan or new job lined up.

In the first few days afterward, I'll admit I spent a few nights wide awake, *curled up in bed worrying* and wondering, *Did I just make the biggest mistake of my life?* Change is hard, and when you take a leap like that, it's natural to feel scared. I had moments where I felt overwhelmed, confused, and just plain terrified of the unknown.

But amid all that fear and chaos, something **amazing** happened too. I began to feel a tiny spark of power flicker to life inside me—the same spark that had pushed me to write that letter in the first place. Each day after I left that job, I woke up feeling a little *lighter.* I felt proud of myself for the first time in ages. I hadn't just walked away from a job; I had ***cut off the doubts and fears that were keeping me small.***

Looking back now, I realize that moment was the first time I truly stepped into my own empowerment. By choosing my voice and my dreams over somebody else's definition of success, I proved to myself how strong I really was. It wasn't easy—honestly, it was one of the toughest times in my life—but I wouldn't trade it for anything.

That experience taught me that empowerment isn't given to us; it's something we claim. And once you claim even a little bit of it, it changes you. I began to respect myself so much more, because I finally saw what I was capable of. And you know what? Over time, the people in my life started to respect me more as well, because I was ***finally respecting myself.***

Understanding Empowerment

So, what does it actually mean to *embrace your personal power?* I used to think being empowered meant you had to be the loudest person in the room or that you needed to have all the answers. Thank goodness, that's not true at all!

Empowerment, as I've learned, is more like a steady, quiet confidence that starts from deep inside. It's that inner knowing that **you are strong, capable, and deserving of respect**—no matter what anyone else might say or think. It's not about bossing others around or trying to control everything; it's about being the boss of ***your own life.***

When you tap into your personal power, it's like flipping on a light switch inside yourself. Suddenly, you stand a little taller. You speak a little clearer. You carry yourself with a sense of self-respect that other people can *feel*.

And here's the beautiful thing: when you respect yourself, you set the standard for how others should treat you. In my case, once I started valuing my own voice and worth, I noticed I stopped putting up with people who brought me down. I naturally began surrounding myself with people who **lifted me up** and celebrated the real me. Those who only wanted the quiet, people-pleasing version of me either had to adjust or eventually drifted out of my life—and that was okay.

Embracing your strength can truly transform your life in so many ways. It builds a genuine confidence—not the fake "I'm fine, everything's fine" kind, but the real, deep-down trust in yourself that doesn't get easily shaken by a bad day or a bit of criticism. It also brings a new level of peace, because you're no longer constantly second-guessing yourself or seeking approval from every direction (or from, say, *everyone and their cat*).

You start to trust yourself more. You give yourself permission to go after what you truly want, and to say "no" to what you don't. That's huge, my friend! Whether it's setting a boundary with a relative who's pushing too hard, or finally signing up for that class you were nervous about—empowerment shows up in both big and small ways. Each time you honor that inner strength, you reinforce your own worth.

Now, I want to be super honest with you: stepping into your power doesn't mean you'll never feel fear or doubt again. Oh boy, you *will*—trust me, I still do sometimes. But empowerment means you don't let that fear or doubt run the show. You might acknowledge it ("Okay, I see you, fear.") and then choose to move forward anyway, even if it's with tiny baby steps. It's about owning your choices and believing that you can handle whatever comes your way. And guess what? You can. Think about it—you've already made it through every single one of your hardest days up to now. That track record is pretty amazing, and it shows that you're stronger than you even realize.

Reflection & Journaling Prompts

Let's turn the focus to you now, lovely, because your story matters just as much as mine. I invite you to grab your writing implements *(or just sit and reflect)* as we explore a few gentle questions together.

Remember, there are no right or wrong answers here. This isn't a test or homework. Think of it like we're just chatting over coffee and I casually asked you these things. Write down whatever comes to your mind and heart. You might be surprised by what you discover about your own strength and courage.

• • •

Remember a Moment of Strength: *Can you think of a time in your life when you surprised yourself with your own bravery or strength? Maybe you stood up for yourself in a tough situation, or tackled something you didn't think you could do. What happened, and how did it feel afterward? Try to relive that proud moment on paper and notice what it tells you about your capabilities.*

Exploring Personal Power: *What does the phrase "personal power" mean to you? Jot down any words, feelings, or images that pop up. Is it a feeling, an action, or maybe it reminds you of a person who inspires you? Describe how being fully in your power would look and feel in your everyday life.*

Identifying a Limiting Belief: *We all have those pesky little voices of doubt. What is one limiting belief about yourself that has been holding you back from feeling truly confident? (For example, "I'm not talented enough," or "I always mess things up.") Write it down, and then ask yourself: where do you think that belief came from? How has it influenced some of your choices up to now?*

Boundaries and Confidence: *Think about a situation or relationship where you know you need to set a healthier boundary to protect your well-being. What would setting that boundary look like, and what's one small step you could take toward making it happen? How might your life change if you respected your needs in that way?*

Your Empowered Future Self: *Close your eyes and imagine yourself five or ten years from now, living your most empowered, fulfilling life. What are you doing? Who is around you? How do you feel when you wake up in the morning? Let yourself dream big and describe that future in as much detail as you can. This vision is you at your most powerful—take a moment to get acquainted with her!*

Take your time with these prompts. You don't have to tackle them all at once. Maybe pick one that speaks to you today, and come back to the others later. The goal here is to gently dive into your own experiences and feelings about empowerment. Even just writing a few sentences can spark insights that make your inner light shine a little brighter.

The "Cut It Off" Release: Cutting the Ribbon to Empowerment

Alright, now that you've done some deep reflecting, let's move on to one of my favorite rituals. It's time to symbolically **cut off whatever is holding you back** from your power—*literally!* By now, you know I love a meaningful gesture, so let's do a little ribbon-cutting ceremony to mark your step into empowerment.

1. **Prepare Your Ribbon:** Grab a piece of ribbon, string, or yarn (if you don't have one handy, even a long strip of paper can work). It

doesn't need to be very long—just enough that you can tie it between two objects and then cut it. If possible, tie the ribbon across a doorway or between two sturdy pieces of furniture (like the backs of two chairs) so that it's stretched out horizontally at about chest height. If that's not practical, you can hold the ribbon taut with one hand on each end *(or ask a friend to help by holding one end)*—whatever works, as long as you have a ribbon "line" you can cut through.

2. **Give It Meaning:** Take a quiet moment to **set an intention** for this ribbon. Imagine that on *your* side of the ribbon is everything that's been holding you back—your fears, doubts, or the expectations that have weighed you down. On the other side of the ribbon is the *new, empowered you*—the you who trusts herself and stands confidently in her strength. You might even whisper or think of specific things as you look at the ribbon, like, *"On this side I've been afraid to speak up,"* and *"On that side is me using my voice without fear."*

3. **Cut the Ribbon *(Cut off the doubt)*:** Take a deep breath and pick up a pair of scissors *(carefully!)*. Now, just like at a grand opening ceremony, ***snip that ribbon***. As you cut through it, imagine you're slicing through the barrier of fear or doubt in your life. You can say something out loud as you cut—maybe a phrase like, *"I am cutting off what holds me back and stepping into my power."* Go ahead and be as dramatic as you want with this—sometimes a big, bold gesture makes the moment feel more meaningful. Cut the ribbon completely so there's a clear opening in front of you.

4. **Step Forward:** Now step through where that ribbon used to be. Physically move yourself into that open space you've created. This is a symbolic step into your empowered life. Take a moment to stand there and breathe. Notice how it feels to be on the other side of that barrier. Do you feel a little lighter? A bit proud? Maybe even excited? Let yourself feel all of it—you just declared a new beginning for yourself.

5. **Mark the Moment *(Optional)*:** Decide what you want to do with the pieces of the ribbon you cut. You could throw them away as a way of saying "good riddance" to whatever was holding you back. Or you might keep a piece of the ribbon in your journal or jewelry box as a reminder of this moment when you chose *you*. Do whatever

feels right to you. The important thing is that you recognize: *you had the courage to cut through what was holding you back.*

It might seem like a simple exercise, but these symbolic gestures carry a lot of emotional weight. By literally cutting through a ribbon that represented your fears or doubts, you're telling your mind and heart, *I am done letting these things hold me back.* You're training yourself to release what doesn't serve you and to make room for a new, empowered you.

And if those old doubts try to creep back later *(which happens to the best of us)*, you can remember this little ceremony. Picture yourself standing on the other side of that cut ribbon and remind yourself, *"Nope, I cut that off and left it behind."* You took your power back, one snip at a time, and that is something no one can take away from you.

Creative Exercise: Personal Empowerment Manifesto

Now that you've symbolically stepped into your power by cutting that ribbon, let's fill that new space with something positive and uplifting. This is where we get a little creative and *a whole lot* bold! I invite you to create your very own ***Personal Empowerment Manifesto.***

Don't let the word *"manifesto"* scare you—think of it as a heartfelt declaration or a love letter to your own strength. It's a statement *(or a series of statements)* about who you are when you're standing tall in your personal power, and how you promise to honor that power every day. It's just for you, by you, so you can make it as unique and heartfelt as you want. A will add here a full page for you.

Here are some steps to guide you in crafting your Personal Empowerment Manifesto:

1. **Set the Scene:** Find a comfortable, inspiring spot to write. Maybe curl up with a cup of tea, light your favorite candle, or play an empowering song in the background. Do whatever puts you in the mood to celebrate you.

2. **Give It a Title:** Start by writing a bold title at the top of the page bellow. It could be something like "My Empowerment Manifesto," "Promises to Myself," or even simply *"I Am Strong."* Pick a title that makes you smile or gives you a little thrill of pride when you see it—think of it as your personal motto for courage.

3. **Write Your Power Statements:** Now, write out a few statements or bullet points that affirm your strength and intentions. Use "I" statements (since this is you talking to yourself). For example, you might write things like: *"I am worthy of respect," "I speak up for myself with confidence," "I choose to follow my own path, not the one others expect of me,"* or *"I am brave and I handle challenges with grace."* Think about the values and truths that make you feel powerful, and put those into words.

4. **Include Your Boundaries:** It's helpful to include a line or two about boundaries, since protecting your energy is a big part of staying empowered. You could add something like, *"I have the right to say no without feeling guilty,"* or *"I only allow supportive, positive people into my inner circle."* This is your reminder that setting boundaries is not just okay—it's essential for your well-being and confidence.

5. **Make It Yours:** Feel free to decorate or stylize your manifesto however you like. Draw little doodles or stars, use colorful markers, or keep it clean and simple—whatever makes it resonate with you.

The goal is to make this manifesto something that *speaks* to you. You want to feel a spark of joy or determination whenever you look at it.

6. **Keep It Close:** Put your manifesto somewhere you'll see it often. Maybe tape it to your mirror, tuck it in your journal, or save a photo of it on your phone. Whenever you're feeling a bit low or uncertain, read over your words. Let your own powerful statements remind you of who you are and the strength you carry.

By creating this manifesto, you're essentially building a shield of positive beliefs to protect and nurture your personal power. Every time you read or say those words, you're reinforcing that sense of empowerment. It's like watering a plant—each affirmation or promise you've written is a little drop of water that helps your confidence grow stronger and flourish.

Self-Care Strategies

Stepping into your personal power is an ongoing journey, and even the most confident among us *(yes, even the fierce queens!)* need to refill their cup from time to time. Think of the following self-care strategies as your best friend *(hi, that's me!)* gently reminding you to take care of *you*, so your confidence stays bright and your spirit stays strong. Here are some of my go-to tips for keeping that empowered feeling alive in everyday life:

- **Speak to Yourself Kindly:** Pay attention to that voice in your head and make sure she's talking to you like a friend, not a critic. Practice speaking to yourself the way you would to someone you love. When you catch yourself thinking something harsh, pause and reframe it into a kinder thought. For example, instead of "I really messed up," you might tell yourself, *"I'm human and I'm learning—it's okay."* Treating yourself with compassion builds up your inner strength and trust in yourself.

- **Practice Saying "No" *(Without Guilt)*:** This one can be tough, but it's so important. Every time you say "yes" to something that isn't right for you or that stretches you too thin, you're actually saying "no" to yourself and what you truly need. Remember, you are allowed to politely decline requests or invitations that don't feel aligned with your well-being. You don't have to give a big explanation either. Your time and energy are yours, and protecting them is a form of self-respect. Saying "no" when you need to is actually saying "yes" to yourself.

- **Surround Yourself with Positivity:** You don't have to walk this path alone. Choose to spend time with people who uplift and inspire you. Think about which friends or family members make you feel strong and happy, and which ones leave you feeling drained or unsure of yourself. It might be time to set gentle boundaries with the latter *(remember, you have that right)*. Also, fill your world with positive influences—maybe a podcast that motivates you during your commute, a bookshelf full of empowering stories, or even uplifting quotes stuck on your fridge. Curate an environment that reminds you of your strength and keeps you looking forward.

- **Celebrate Your Wins—*Big and Small*:** Make it a habit to acknowledge and celebrate your accomplishments, no matter how tiny they may seem. Did you speak up in that meeting even though your heart was racing? Girl, that's a win—celebrate it! Did you finally take a day off to rest because you were running on empty? That's a win too. Every time you recognize your own progress, you reinforce the belief that you are capable and strong. Some people I know keep a little "success journal" where they jot down one thing they're proud of each day. It's such a lovely way to keep track of your wins and give yourself credit where it's due.

- **Recharge Your Body and Mind:** We've all heard it before, but here it is again: taking care of your physical well-being makes a *huge* difference in how you feel emotionally. Try to get the sleep your body needs *(yes, I'm looking at those midnight Netflix binges—no judgment, I've been there too!)*. Move your body in ways that feel good—maybe that's a yoga session, a dance party in your kitchen, a long walk in nature, or a fun workout class. And nourish yourself with food that gives you energy and strength. When your body feels cared for, you'll find it so much easier to face challenges and stay confident.

- **Keep Learning and Growing:** Empowerment is also about growth. Is there a skill you've wanted to learn or something new you've been curious about? Go for it! Sign up for that class, watch some how-to videos, or start a little project on the side. Learning new things not only boosts your confidence, it also reminds you that you're capable of change and adaptation. It's pretty hard to feel stuck when you're busy expanding your horizons—even if it's just learning a new recipe or picking up a few phrases in a new language. Every bit of growth is proof to yourself that you can do things you've never done before.

Remember, these ideas aren't items on a chore list. They're ***acts of love toward yourself.*** So pick one or two that resonate and try to weave them gently into your routine. Even small, consistent acts of self-care can keep that empowerment fire of yours burning bright.

Affirmations for Strength & Empowerment

I'm a big believer in the power of affirmations—those positive statements we repeat to remind ourselves of our worth and potential. At first, I'll admit, I felt *super* silly talking to my mirror and saying nice things to myself. But over time, those words started to sink in and helped rewrite some of the negative stories I used to tell myself. Think of affirmations as little love notes to your soul, teaching your mind a new, empowering script.

Here are some of my favorite affirmations for strength and personal power. You can say them in your head, jot them in your journal, or speak them out loud *(my personal favorite is belting them out in the car where no one can hear me!)*. As you say each one, really let the words land—remember, they're about you:

- *I am strong, capable, and resilient.*
- *My voice matters, and I deserve to be heard.*
- *I honor my needs and set healthy boundaries without guilt.*
- *I trust myself to make the best decisions for my life.*
- *I am worthy of respect and love–from others and from myself.*
- *Each challenge I face is an opportunity for me to grow and shine.*
- *I stand in my power and am proud of who I am becoming.*
- *I release any doubt about my worth–I know I am more than enough.*

Feel free to tweak these or come up with your own affirmations that resonate with you. The key is that the words feel true (or at least feel *possible*) to you, even if you're still working on believing them fully. Every time you repeat an affirmation, you're planting a seed. With time and practice, those seeds will grow into new beliefs and realities that reflect the powerful, capable person you truly are.

As we wrap up this chapter, I want you to take a moment and really soak in how far you've come. Empowerment isn't a destination; it's a journey—one you're already on, one brave step at a time. I am *so* proud of you for diving into this chapter and for every bit of effort you're investing in yourself.

Remember, I'm right here cheering you on, every step of the way. You are stronger than you know, and the world is so lucky to have your light in it.

Keep shining, and keep owning that power, beautiful. You've got this!

I am the author of my own story,
fierce in my truth,
fearless in my growth,
and unstoppable in my power
I rise, I thrive,
and I claim
the extraordinary life that I deserve.

9

New Beginnings

Hello again, my amazing friend! Can you believe we're here at Chapter 9 already? It feels like just yesterday we were taking that first brave step together, and now look at how far you've come. I'm so **proud** of the work you've done in these pages—all the honest reflections, the difficult let-go's, the little victories. This chapter is a special one; it's our final chapter *(...more or less, ahhh)* in this guided journey. But don't think of it as an ending—think of it as a **grand beginning.** In these next few pages, we're going to celebrate your growth, tie up any loose ends of negativity, and get you all set to step forward into the beautiful new chapter of your life that ***you*** will continue to write.

Take a deep breath with me. In...and out. This moment is a bit like standing at sunrise after a long night—there's a gentle light on the horizon, full of hope and new possibilities. 🌅 You've done so much inner work to reach this dawn. Now, Chapter 9 is about **embracing your new beginning** with an open heart. And you know me by now—of course I have one more story to share about a turning point in my own life that taught me about new beginnings. So grab a cozy seat and maybe a glass of "wine", and let's have one more heart-to-heart. Ready? Here we go.

Finding Purpose in Sharing My Story

Not too long ago, I found myself on the cusp of a new beginning that I never imagined for myself. I had spent a couple of years doing the hard work of healing—much of the same work you've been doing: cutting off toxic ties, learning to set boundaries, practicing gratitude, and discovering my own strength. I had emerged from those struggles feeling lighter and more confident. But then a quiet, persistent little voice inside started saying, ***"Clara, maybe you can help someone else with what you've learned."***

At first, I'll admit, I **shushed** that voice. Who was I to guide anyone? I wasn't a therapist or a life coach or some all-knowing guru. I was just a woman who had a collection of scarred-over wounds and hard-won lessons. The idea of sharing my deeply personal stories in a book or journal terrified me. I remember opening my laptop one evening, staring at a blank document titled *"Cut It Off—Journal Idea,"* and immediately closing it again. *Nope, not doing that*, I thought. My heart was pounding at the mere thought of writing down my experiences for other eyes to see.

For weeks, I wrestled with self-doubt. Every time I considered starting, a hundred anxious questions swirled in my mind: *What if I'm not good enough to do this? What if nobody cares about my story? What if I open up and people judge me for it?* It felt safer to keep my journey to myself. After all, I had already grown so much personally—couldn't I just leave it at that? Why risk the vulnerability of putting it out into the world?

Then came the moment that changed everything. I was having coffee with an old friend—someone who had seen me at my lowest, back when I was stuck in a toxic situation I hadn't yet cut off. She noticed how different I seemed now. She said, **"Clara, you just look *free*. I can't explain it, but something about you is so much lighter and happier."** Her words made my eyes well up, because I *felt* exactly what she was describing. I told her a bit about the journey I had been on—how I learned to let go of the things that were hurting me and started finding myself again. I even shyly mentioned that I had thought about writing a guided journal to help others do the same, but that I was scared to start.

My friend reached across the table and squeezed my hand. *"You **have** to do it,"* she said. *"Even if it helps one other person feel what you feel now, it will be worth it. I'd have given anything to have a guide like that when I was struggling."* The sincerity in her voice and the warmth in her eyes sparked something in me. At that moment, I felt a **shift**—as if the fear was still there, but a newfound sense of purpose was suddenly stronger.

That night, I went home, opened my laptop again, and began to write. This time, the words started flowing. I wrote about the pain of past wounds, the relief of letting go, the awkward but freeing process of learning to say "no," the joy of rediscovering creativity, and the power I found in myself when I chose my own path. Some chapters made me laugh as I typed *(yes, I really did do a goofy happy dance alone in my living room after setting a hard boundary one time!)*, and some chapters made me cry remembering how far I've come. But through it all, I kept imagining **you**—the woman who might read these words someday. I imagined you holding this journal, maybe feeling a bit stuck or hurt or hopeful, and I wrote to you like the friend I wished I'd had beside me during my toughest days.

Hitting "save" on the first full draft of *Cut It Off* was one of the most emotional moments of my life. I sat there in a mixture of disbelief, pride, and vulnerability hangover *(that woozy feeling you get after sharing something deeply personal)*. Part of me still worried—oh boy, did I worry—but a much larger part of me felt **alive** and **aligned** with my purpose. I realized that all those twists and turns, all those things I had to cut off in my life, had led me right here: to a new beginning where my pain could blossom into something meaningful for others.

That decision to share my story—to start *this* very journal you're holding—was a major turning point for me. It taught me that sometimes the **scariest** paths lead to the most fulfilling destinations. I learned that a new beginning often asks us to step forward **before** we feel completely ready. If I had waited until I felt "ready" or 100% confident, well... you wouldn't be reading this now because I'd still be hiding from my calling. Instead, I took a leap of faith, trusting that my heart was in the right place. And here we are together.

So why am I telling you this? Because as we stand together at the end of Chapter 9, *you* are on the cusp of your own leap of faith. You've been transforming and healing through these chapters, and now a new chapter in **your** life is about to begin. I want you to know that I understand how exciting and scary that can be, all at once. But trust me, my friend: if you feel that little tug in your heart, that whisper urging you toward something new—whether it's a fresh start, a brave decision, or simply embracing a new attitude—**listen to it.** Honor it. Even if you feel nervous. **Especially** if you feel nervous. Sometimes that flutter in your chest is a sign that something truly beautiful is waiting on the other side of fear.

Embracing Your Next Chapter

Take a moment with me now to reflect on **your** journey. Think back to why you picked up this journal in the first place. You had an instinct that something in your life needed to change—that there was some negativity to cut off or some part of yourself waiting to bloom. Over these chapters, you've dug deep. You've identified toxic influences, confronted past wounds, learned to be more present, set healthy boundaries, rekindled your creativity, embraced change, nurtured gratitude, and stepped into your personal power. Wow! ✹ **That is amazing.** Please pause here and give yourself credit for every insight gained and every step forward you've taken. You deserve a giant hug for all of it—so consider yourself lovingly squeezed by me right now. *I mean it!* 🤗

Now, with all that behind you, a question emerges: **What's next?** What will you do with the open space you've created in your heart and life? This is the exciting part, my dear. When we cut off what no longer serves us, we make room for **new beginnings.** It's like clearing out a garden of weeds—now you have rich soil ready for fresh flowers of your choosing. What will you plant in this next season of your life?

It's okay if you don't have all the answers. New beginnings can be a little daunting precisely because they're new and unknown. You might feel a mix of enthusiasm and uncertainty as you think about life after this journal. That's perfectly normal. Embracing your next chapter doesn't mean you have everything figured out; it simply means you're **open** to growth and committed to continuing on the path you've started. It means carrying forward the lessons and self-love you've been cultivating here.

One thing I want you to remember is that ***you are the author of your own story.*** You've proven that by being the co-author of this journal with me—every prompt you answered, every exercise you completed, you added your own words and experiences to these pages. *That* is huge. It shows that you have the power to shape your narrative moving forward. Maybe in your next chapter you'll pursue a dream that you once pushed aside. Maybe you'll build healthier relationships that uplift you. Maybe you'll continue a newfound habit like journaling or meditation to keep nurturing your well-being. Whatever it is, it will be **your choice** and **your creation.**

Let's do a few gentle journaling prompts to help you envision and step into this new beginning. There's no right or wrong way to respond—just let your heart speak.

• • •

Reflect on the journey you've taken through Chapters **1-8**. *What are the three biggest changes or insights you've gained about yourself or your life? Write them down and acknowledge how far you've come. What do these insights mean for you moving forward?*

When you imagine the "next chapter" of your life unfolding after you finish this book, what do you see? *Describe it as vividly as you can. Consider how you want to feel each day, who you want to be around, and what kinds of things you want to spend your time on. Don't worry about being practical—dream big and focus on what genuinely lights you up.*

What is one new beginning you are ready to embrace right now? *It could be a new mindset (e.g. "I am going to be kinder to myself"), a new opportunity (perhaps starting a class or hobby, or saying yes to an adventure), or a new chapter in a relationship (setting healthier dynamics, or opening your heart to new people). Why does this new beginning matter to you, and how does it make you feel when you think about it?*

Consider the space you've created by cutting off negative influences. What positive things do you want to invite into that space? Maybe it's more self-confidence, peace, love, creativity, or a specific experience like travel or a career change. List a few things you intend to welcome into your life as you move forward.

Take your time with these prompts. This is your moment to really imagine the life that awaits you and set some gentle intentions. When you're ready, let's move on to one more special ritual together—our final "Cut It Off" exercise in this book. I've saved something a little different and extra meaningful for last.

The Final "Cut It Off" Ritual: Breaking the Chains of the Past

You're a pro at our "Cut It Off" rituals by now, and I hope you've found empowerment in those symbolic acts of cutting and releasing. For our grand finale, we're going to do a completely original ritual that symbolizes breaking free from any lingering negativity and truly embracing your fresh start. This one is a bit like a mini ceremony to mark your transformation. And don't worry—it's simple and actually pretty fun to do!

What you'll need: A few strips of paper *(3 to 5 strips is a good start)*, a pen, some tape (or a stapler), and a pair of scissors. Optional: if you have some ribbon or string and prefer to use that instead of paper, that can work too.

1. **Identify your links:** Take those strips of paper and on each one, write down something you are *so ready* to cut off as you move into your new chapter. Think of any last remnants of fear, doubt, or old labels that you haven't fully shaken off yet. For example, one strip might say "fear of failure," another might say "negative body image," or "that toxic friendship," or "guilt about X." Be honest with yourself about anything that still feels like it's holding you back, even a little. Each strip will represent one thing you're releasing. *(If you're using a piece of string or ribbon instead of paper strips, you can tie a small knot for each thing you name, or even attach a tiny piece of paper with the words to the string.)*

2. **Create a paper chain *(your old chains)*:** Now, let's physically symbolize those old ties. Take one paper strip, form it into a loop (with the writing on the inside or outside, your choice), and tape or staple the ends together. Then take the next strip, thread it through the first loop, and tape its ends to form the second link of a chain. Continue with each strip until all your written "old stuff" is linked together in a chain of paper loops. Take a moment to look at this chain you've created. These are the chains of the past that have at times bound you with negativity or fear. You have named them, and there they are—visible and separate from you.

3. **Set your intention:** Hold that paper chain in your hands gently. Take a deep breath and say (out loud or in your mind): *"I am releasing these old chains. They do not define me or control me anymore."* You can speak directly to each link if you want: "Goodbye, fear," "Goodbye, self-doubt," etc. Use whatever words feel empowering to you. The key is to declare that you are **done** letting these things hold you back. This is a moment of acknowledgment. You might even feel a bit of gratitude toward these "chains"—strange as it sounds—because they taught you lessons and made you who you are. But you no longer need them, so you're kindly but firmly letting them go now.

4. **Cut the chain:** Here comes the satisfying part! Take your scissors,

and one by one, cut through each paper loop of the chain. ***Snip... snap... snip!*** ✂ With each cut, watch that link fall away from the chain. Imagine and **feel** the ties truly breaking. You are literally cutting the chain of whatever has been weighing you down. As you cut, you can say a simple phrase like, *"I cut you off,"* or *"I am free,"* or even *"not anymore!"*—whatever resonates with you. Take your time with it. Notice what it feels like as you sever each link. Do you feel a sense of relief? Power? Maybe a little sadness or tenderness? It's all okay. Let yourself experience this fully. By the time you've cut all the links, you'll have a pile of separate pieces of paper instead of a chain. Those represent the old burdens no longer binding you together.

5. **Dispose and cleanse:** Just as we've done before, choose how you want to dispose of these remnants. You can toss the pile of paper links in the trash, knowing they belong in the garbage bin of your past. If it's safe and you prefer a more dramatic flourish, you might even carefully burn them (in a fireplace or fire-safe pot) and watch the smoke carry away the last traces. Or you could bury the pieces in the ground as a way to lay the past to rest. Do whatever feels right and ceremonious to you. As you do it, take a long, deep breath and on your exhale imagine all of those old energies whooshing out of your life for good. *Good riddance!*

6. **Celebrate your freedom:** Finally, mark this moment of freedom with a tiny celebration. You just broke the chains that once held you back—how incredible is that? You might place a hand on your heart and quietly say, *"I am free"* or *"I am proud of myself."* Or, if you're anything like me, you might crank up a feel-good song and do a little ***happy dance*** right there *(yes, jumping around in your living room totally counts!)*. Do whatever joyful action symbolizes *victory* to you. Let yourself feel the weight lifted. You have cut off what you no longer need, and you're stepping forward as a stronger, freer you.

How do you feel after doing that? Take a moment to sit with whatever is coming up for you. You might feel lighter, or emotional, or a bit of both. All of it is valid. If you're tearing up, allow those tears—they can be tears of release and relief. If you're smiling, let that smile spread. If you're in disbelief that you actually did all this, that's okay too. **You did it.**

Go ahead and **write down any feelings or thoughts** that bubbled up during this ritual. This is your space to process and remember this moment. There's no prompt here except to honor *your experience* of this exercise.

...

Deep breath in, and out. **Wow.** This was a big moment, my friend. You've engaged in a powerful act of self-liberation. Symbolic rituals like this might seem simple, but they carry a lot of meaning. By breaking that chain, you've sent a clear message to your mind, heart, and body: *I am moving on*. I hope you feel as proud of yourself as I feel of you right now.

Before we conclude our journey in this book, I want to guide you through one last gentle ceremony—a closing reflection to truly honor how far you've come and to set your eyes on the road ahead.

Reflective Closing Ceremony: Your Story Continues 📖

Imagine this scene: It's a calm evening, and you're sitting by a warm little fire on a beach, just as the sun is setting. The sky is painted with hues of orange and lavender, and each gentle wave that meets the shore seems to whisper **closure** and **renewal**. In your hand, you hold this journal—its pages filled with your truths, your struggles, your victories, your heart. The fire crackles softly, and you know it's time to say goodbye to this guided journey and hello to a new dawn in your life.

If you like, you can create a bit of this scene in real life for our closing ceremony. Maybe light a candle to symbolize that little fire. Play some soft music that soothes you. Or simply sit in a quiet, comfortable spot with a cup of tea. Do anything that makes this moment feel special and reflective for you.

Now, gently close your eyes (after you read this paragraph). Take a few slow breaths. ***Inhale*** peace, ***exhale*** any remaining tension. Feel the weight of the book in your hands—it's a testament to all the inner work you've done. When you open your eyes, perhaps flip back through some of the pages of this journal. Notice the words you've written, the emotions spilled out, the dreams sketched in margins, maybe even the tear stains or doodles here and there. That is the **tangible proof** of your healing journey. *That is you*, poured out on paper with courage and honesty.

Now turn to this section again and consider: as this Chapter 9 comes to an end, what does it mean for **you?** Endings can be bittersweet, but every ending in life is also a beginning in disguise. This closing ceremony is not really about "the end" at all—it's about honoring your **new beginning.** The guided part of your journey may be concluding, **but your story is far from over.** In fact, a whole new chapter is unfolding, one that you will author.

I have a little secret to share: I intentionally made this journal only 9 chapters long, because Chapter 10 belongs to *you*. That's right—**you are the author of Chapter 10.** Consider Chapter 10 the unwritten chapter—the blank pages that follow this one are for you to continue writing your story, in this book and beyond. You don't need my prompts or exercises anymore; you have your own inner guidance to follow now. How empowering is that? The pen (or pencil or crayon or keyboard...) is in *your* hand, and you get to decide what happens next in the adventure of your life.

Let's seal this moment with an intention or a promise to yourself. Take a second to reflect: *What promise do I want to carry forward from this journey?* It could be something like, "I promise to treat myself with kindness and respect," or "I intend to continue letting go of what hurts me and welcoming what heals me," or even *"I vow to embrace new experiences even if they scare me a little."* If one comes to mind, hold that promise in your heart. You might even speak it aloud or write it on the inside cover of this book, turning it into a personal contract with yourself. This intention is your guiding star for Chapter 10 and beyond.

Lastly, let's cultivate a feeling of **gratitude**. Gratitude for yourself—for the strength you've shown and the effort you've invested in your well-being. Gratitude for the lessons learned (even the tough ones). And gratitude for the unknown future, trusting that it holds good things in store for you. Take a moment to whisper a "thank you"—to the universe, to God if you're spiritual, or simply to yourself. *Thank you, self, for showing up and doing this. I deserve the happiness I'm working toward.*

As we conclude this closing ceremony, I want you to picture one more thing: Imagine a beautiful door in front of you. On this side of the door is everything you've released—all the pages of this journal, all the pain and doubts that you've poured out and cut off. On the other side of the door is a bright, open field under a morning sky—it represents the rest of your life, fresh and inviting. When you're ready, see yourself turning the knob and **stepping through** that door. Feel the sunlight of that new day on your face. You're lighter now, and you carry with you only what serves you: hope, self-love, wisdom, courage. Take a deep breath and step forward, one foot and then the other, until you are fully in that open field of your future. The door gently closes behind you, not as a loss, but as a completion. You can always open it and peek at the past if you need a reminder of how far you've come, but it no longer confines you. You are free to roam and create in this new space.

Open your eyes (if you had them closed for visualization). Hi there, bright soul. 😊 You made it. This is the end of the guided journal, **but the beginning of your next chapter.** I want you to know, from the deepest part of my heart, that it has been an honor to walk beside you through these pages. Even though I may not know you by name, I feel connected to you and so proud of you. You've shown up for *yourself*, which is truly the bravest, most beautiful thing you could do.

Whenever you need, remember that I'm still here in these pages cheering you on. You can revisit any chapter, any prompt, any story whenever you want a friendly voice or a reminder of your own strength. But also trust that you have everything you need within you to keep growing and healing. ***You are strong. You are capable. You are worthy of every bit of happiness coming your way.***

So go on, my friend—get out there and write Chapter 10 of your life. Fill it with authenticity, with love, with adventure, with you. I know it's going to be extraordinary, because the author is extraordinary.

9.5

A Open Letter With All My Love

My heart's dearest friend,

Here we are at the final part, and I can hardly believe how far you've come. It feels like just yesterday you were opening to the first page, maybe with a bit of uncertainty about what you'd find. Now look at you—lighter, stronger, and glowing with the growth you've nurtured in these pages. Take a moment and let that sink in—*you did this.* You showed up for yourself again and again, and that is something to celebrate with all your heart!

As I sit here reflecting on everything you've uncovered and released, I am filled with so much pride in you. I know there were days when this journey felt heavy—moments when a prompt brought tears or when you had to face a truth you'd kept buried. But you persisted with such courage.

There were also moments of triumph—the laughter that bubbled up when you felt a weight lift off your shoulders, the breakthroughs where a new understanding dawned, the quiet sigh of relief when you realized you were healing bit by bit. Through every high and every low, you kept going. You bravely *cut off* the thoughts, fears, and habits that no longer serve you, pruning away old pain to make space for new, beautiful growth. Please, take pride in that. What you have done is nothing short of incredible.

This might be the last page of our guided journey together, but it's definitely not the end of *your* story—far from it. Think of this moment as a warm hug at a crossroads, a pause to honor how far you've come before you continue on your own beautiful path. You have so many new insights, tools, and a whole lot more self-love packed into your suitcase for the journey ahead. I have every bit of faith in you. I've seen your heart and your strength shine through on these pages, and I know you're going to keep blooming in ways you can't even imagine yet.

From here on out, you are the author of your own story. In fact, you always have been—I was just the friend walking beside you for a chapter or two. Now the pen is in your hands, and Chapter 10 (and every chapter after) is yours to write.

Fill it with authenticity, with love, with adventure—fill it with everything that makes you uniquely *you*. Write it boldly and without fear, with the courage to chase whatever lights you up and the wisdom to know you deserve every bit of joy along the way. And whatever happens, remember that you get to decide how your story unfolds. *Your life is your book, and you are the author, the hero, and the editor all at once.*

As you step forward into this next chapter of your life, carry with you the knowledge of how strong and capable you are. Whenever you start to doubt yourself (because we all do sometimes), I want you to remember this journey. Remember the fears you faced and the burdens you set down. Flip back through these pages if you need to and re-read your own words—the hopes, the truths, the victories big and small that you've recorded. Let them remind you of the fire inside and how far you've come.

That strength and wisdom isn't just on the pages; it's in you. It's always been in you.

I wish I could reach through this page and give you a big, proud hug right now. I hope you can feel how sincerely I mean it when I say I am so proud of you.

It has been one of the greatest honors of my life to be a friend and guide in your story up to this point. Thank you for trusting me with your vulnerabilities and your hopes. Thank you for allowing me to walk beside you for a while. I've been continually inspired by your openness, your honesty, and your determination to grow.

Now, as you go out and continue writing your story, I want you to carry one truth above all in your heart: *You are worthy of the happiness and peace you seek, and you have the power to create it.* The pages ahead are blank, ready for the next beautiful chapter of *you*. Fill them with new discoveries, new beginnings, and the kind of love and freedom you've been working so hard to welcome into your life.

And if you ever find yourself in a hard moment—when the sky gets a little cloudy and you're not sure what comes next—remember that you've made it through storms before, and you've always found your way. You are never truly back at square one; you're standing on the strength of all the chapters you've already written. So take a deep breath, feel your feet planted firmly on the ground, and know that you have everything you need inside you to face whatever comes. You've proven that to yourself over and over.

I believe in you, my friend. I believe in your resilience, your kindness, and the light that you carry. I'm cheering you on, now and always. In my mind I'm raising a coffee mug *"or my glass of wine" (you know I always have one in hand)* to toast *you*—to your courage, your growth, and the journey that lies ahead. Here's to embracing everything that awaits you with an open heart and the unshakable knowledge that you can handle it—whatever "it" may be.

So go on, my dear friend, and write your Chapter 10. Step forward with confidence into that wide-open future you've been preparing for. Trust yourself and the path you're creating. And remember, this isn't goodbye. I am with you in spirit on every page you write from here on out, always whispering encouragement and love.

Your story is just beginning, and I know it's going to be extraordinary—because its author is extraordinary.

With all my love and a hopeful heart,

Clara

10

Chapter 10:

Made in the USA
Monee, IL
04 May 2025

16853536R00096